TODAY's
HOT JOB TARGETS

find careers and cities with big job growth

Michael Farr | *America's Career Expert*

and LAURENCE SHATKIN, PH.D.

Also in JIST's Help in a Hurry Series

- *Overnight Career Choice*
- *Same-Day Resume*
- *Next-Day Job Interview*
- *15-Minute Cover Letter*
- *Seven-Step Job Search*
- *90-Minute College Major Matcher*
- *Next-Day Salary Negotiation*
- *30-Day Job Promotion*
- *One-Hour College Application Essay*

jist Works
America's Career Publisher™

PART OF JIST'S HELP IN A HURRY™ SERIES

TODAY'S HOT JOB TARGETS

© 2007 by JIST Publishing, Inc.

Published by JIST Works, an imprint of JIST Publishing, Inc.
8902 Otis Avenue
Indianapolis, IN 46216-1033
Phone: 1-800-648-JIST   Fax: 1-800-JIST-FAX   E-mail: info@jist.com

Visit our Web site at **www.jist.com** for information on JIST, free job search tips, book chapters, and ordering instructions for our many products!

> Quantity discounts are available for JIST books. Have future editions of JIST books automatically delivered to you on publication through our convenient standing order program. Please call our Sales Department at 1-800-648-5478 for a free catalog and more information.

Acquisitions Editor: Susan Pines
Development Editor: Stephanie Koutek
Interior Designer: Aleata Howard
Page Layout: Trudy Coler, Toi Davis, Marie Kristine Parial-Leonardo
Cover Designer: Katy Bodenmiller
Proofreaders: Paula Lowell, Jeanne Clark
Indexer: Kelly D. Henthorne

Printed in the United States of America
12 11 10 09 08 07   9 8 7 6 5 4 3 2 1

  Library of Congress Cataloging-in-Publication Data
Farr, Michael.
  Today's hot job targets : find careers and cities with big job growth / Michael Farr and Laurence Shatkin.
    p. cm. -- (Help in a hurry)
  Includes index.
  ISBN 978-1-59357-424-6 (alk. paper)
  1. Occupations--United States. 2. Vocational guidance. I. Shatkin, Laurence. II. Title.
  HF5382.5.U5F373 2007
  331.7020973--dc22
                          2007012731

ISBN 978-1-59357-424-6

Identify Red-Hot Jobs for a Sizzling Future

Everybody knows that the health care field is hot these days. But what other jobs are in high demand? What communities are growing rapidly? Are there shortcuts for getting educational credentials? And what's a good strategy for landing a job in the least amount of time? These are questions we can answer—and quickly.

This book is short because we know you're in a hurry. You want quick access to information about the hottest jobs, and you don't want to spend years in school or months sending out resumes. To help you, we assembled a list of 100 particularly hot jobs, packaged the most important facts about them, and provided tips for boosting your skills and igniting your career.

If you are especially pressed for time but not yet committed to a job target, jump right to chapter 4 and do a quick paper-and-pencil exercise that helps you take a look at yourself and your work-related preferences. What you learn can guide you toward the hot jobs that may suit you best. Or if you already have a career goal picked out, start with chapter 6 to learn about shortcuts for upgrading your skills and then follow the advice in chapter 7 for identifying job openings and marketing yourself effectively. Learn proven job-search techniques that produce results quickly.

You may not have to wear oven mitts to turn the pages, but we think you'll find that this book will raise the temperature of your ambitions. So get started!

Contents

Chapter 6: What If I Don't Have the Right Training and Education for a Hot Career?...................................165

Chapter 7: Quick Tips for Getting a Hot Job 171

A Brief Introduction to Using This Book

Some people build their careers at a snail's pace. They are willing to spend years in school and college, sampling various subjects until they find one that really intrigues them enough to pursue as a career. Even after getting an education, they may spend additional years in dead-end jobs, hoping to find an opportunity to get ahead.

This book is not for snails. It's for roadrunners.

You want a career that has a lot of promise for getting ahead quickly. You don't want to spend the better part of a decade preparing for the job. And you don't want to waste time staring at your phone or an empty mailbox, waiting for a job offer to materialize.

So this book helps you focus your thinking quickly and take action. It spotlights 100 jobs that are especially promising now and shows you how to track down job openings using methods that will leave other job hunters in your dust.

Narrowing Down Your Career Choice

Some parts of the U.S. economy are growing at a torrid pace. You know about Health Care. But what about Management, Scientific, and Technical Consulting Services? It's a smaller field, but it's growing *twice* as fast. Chapter 2 will alert you to the fields where the thermostat is set to the max.

Another way to get on the fast track is to move to where the economy is booming. You've probably heard about how fast the Las Vegas area is growing. But a lot of the growth there consists of children and retirees. Do you know where the *workforce* has been growing fastest? Chapter 3 identifies those metro areas where payrolls have been swelling at the fastest rate and provides key facts about them.

By now you may be thinking, "Okay, but you said this book covers *one hundred* hot jobs. How can I find one that's right for me?" In chapter 4 we give you a quick exercise to focus your thinking on hot jobs that are a good match for your personality type.

Some of the jobs you find in the table at the end of chapter 4 may be unfamiliar to you. That's okay; investigate them in chapter 5 anyway. After all, your best friend was once a stranger.

Personality should not be your only consideration when you look for jobs that interest you. You'll also want to think about the work tasks, the working conditions, and the economic rewards. The fact-crammed job snapshots in chapter 5 can help you narrow down your choices.

Taking Action

When you're looking at job snapshots in chapter 5, one of the facts you'll note is the amount of education or training that is normally expected of job candidates. If you're wondering how you'll get the necessary education or training or how you can boost your skills *after* you're hired in order to raise the temperature of your career, chapter 6 has several useful pointers. You'll learn about shortcuts that can cut the time and costs of education.

Of course, all of these decisions and plans are useful only when you actually *get hired*. For the roadrunner's guide to job hunting, turn to chapter 7. You'll learn about the hidden job market and proven strategies for tapping into it—everything from deciding where to make the first phone call to how to make the most of an interview to how to use the Internet most effectively.

This book won't *tell* you what job to look for. It won't *go out* and *get you* a job. But it will make the process easier and faster than you thought possible.

So start taking action now. There's a hot job out there for you; get it before somebody else does.

Chapter 1

Is a Hot Career Right for You?

People who are trying to decide on a career sometimes wonder what factors they should keep in mind. Are skills more important than interests? Should income be the deciding factor? What about the work setting?

No matter how you feel about these factors, one consideration looms above everything else when you plan a career: *You want to be employed.* After all, it will do you no good to choose the "perfect" career, only to find that nobody's hiring.

That's why it's helpful to focus on hot careers—that is, careers that are growing fast and that will have a lot of job openings. We can identify the hot careers thanks to the efforts of the U.S. Department of Labor, which publishes statistics on how fast each career is predicted to grow over the next 10 years and how many job openings can be expected. Of course, the folks who work at the Department of Labor don't have crystal balls. But their projections are based on sophisticated models of how the U.S. economy is changing—for example, which industries are growing or shrinking, the effects of automation and global trade, and the aging of the workforce.

We used the Department of Labor's statistics to create a list of jobs that are especially promising. Every one of them is either growing a lot faster than average or has a very large number of job openings. None of them is shrinking or employing very few workers.

> **Tip:** *For details on how we selected the 100 hot jobs, see the appendix.*

Also, because income seems to matter to just about everyone, we made sure that all of the hot jobs pay better than what the lowest 25 percent of wage-earners get. Finally, we limited the jobs to those that typically require no more than a bachelor's degree for entry. Like the other books in the Help in a Hurry series, this book is about fast solutions, so we did not want to include jobs that require years and years of preparation.

There are hundreds of occupations in the U.S. economy, and you can find some useful books that describe them all in detail. But if your goal is to get hired, doesn't it make sense to focus on the careers where the most hiring is going on?

Just How Hot Are These Jobs?

The 100 jobs described in this book really do offer outstanding opportunities. Whereas the average growth rate for all jobs is 13.0 percent, the jobs in this book have an average growth rate of 17.6 percent. A couple of the jobs are actually growing by more than 50 percent. Think about that: By 2014, those jobs will employ *half again as many* workers as they did in 2004. Another dozen of these jobs are growing by better than one-third.

The Department of Labor projects an average of 68,805 job openings for the 754 occupations it researches, but for the 100 jobs in this book the average is 88,323 job openings. Almost one-third of the occupations in this book will create more than 100,000 job openings each year.

You also don't need to compromise your salary expectations to get a hot job. Whereas the average wage-paying job has earnings of $29,430, the jobs in this book average $34,615. Twenty-one of these jobs pay more than $50,000 per year.

Why Hot Jobs Are Appealing

Hot jobs may be particularly appealing to you for one of the following reasons:

- **You want to find a job in a hurry because something has changed in your life.** Maybe you were laid off, downsized, forced to relocate, or divorced and you're looking for a new career path. Because hot jobs are in demand, they are more likely to provide job openings so you can re-enter the workforce. And many of these are jobs you can qualify for quickly. For one-third of them, workers are hired first and *then* learn the work tasks through on-the-job training that lasts less than a year—maybe only a few days or weeks.

- **You want a steady job with some amount of security.** Of course, no career can guarantee that you'll always be employed, but your chances are better in a hot job. Careers that are growing rapidly need more workers and tend to hold onto the workers who are already employed. Even if you lose your job—for example, let's say your company is being mismanaged and it goes under—your track record in a hot career increases the likelihood that other employers will be eager to take you on.

- **You want a career with chances for advancement.** Most hot jobs are in fields that are growing rapidly and offer chances for climbing up the ladder of responsibility. As you acquire experience and skills in one of these jobs, you may be able to take on higher-level work roles and perhaps get management training.

- **You are planning to get a college education and want to be reasonably assured that your investment will pay off.** College will require you to commit several years and a lot of money. (But be sure to read chapter 6 for suggestions about how to cut college time and expenses.) By choosing a hot career as your target, you improve your chances of finding work in your intended field when you hit the job market a few years from now. The figures for job growth and job openings in this book cover the labor market through 2014, so these hot jobs are not expected to cool off before your graduation day.

Why These Hot Jobs May Not Be for Everybody

Not everybody is going to find an appealing job target in this book. Some people are well advised to go into other careers for a variety of reasons:

- **You have a very specific interest that is not fulfilled in a hot job.** The most obvious example is interest in one of the arts, such as acting, sculpture, or dance. These careers are notorious for being hard to get into and having low or unsteady earnings—but many people have such a love of a particular art form that they will fight the odds. On the other hand, some very narrow career fields have excellent job opportunities because so few people consider them. For example, you might get training to repair and restore antique watches and clocks. This occupation has very few job openings and therefore doesn't belong in this book, but those few jobs are going begging for qualified applicants. There are many other tiny occupations that offer great opportunities for people who are willing to learn the particular skills.

- **You live in a community where many of these jobs are not hot.** We selected the jobs for this book based on national averages, but every community has its particular mix of industries and job seekers. Your community may be dominated by an industry that has little need for the jobs in this book. Or there may be a local abundance of qualified workers competing for these jobs. If you're not willing to relocate, you need to think in terms of what jobs are hottest where you live. Your state's department of labor or employment security can provide you with information on the outlook for specific jobs in your state and metropolitan area. The appendix lists a Web site for accessing this information.

> **Tip:** For a more thorough look at job search, you may want to read Michael Farr's Seven-Step Job Search: Cut Your Job Search Time in Half (JIST Works).

Also keep in mind that aiming for a hot career area is not the only way to get employed; you may simply need to use better methods of looking for work. Chapter 7 of this book has many useful hints about the job search.

For most people, however, the hot jobs in this book include many options worth considering. So go ahead to the next chapter and start thinking about aiming for work in a sector of the economy that is growing rapidly.

Key Points: Chapter 1

- Hot job targets are the jobs that are growing fast and have a lot of openings. They tend to offer the most opportunities to get hired.
- Because hot jobs need lots of workers, they can also offer more security and chances to get ahead.

Chapter 2

A Look at Today's Hot Fields

W hen people make plans for their careers, they usually think in terms of jobs, and jobs are the main focus of this book. However, you should also think in terms of fields (otherwise known as industries), because some are growing much faster than others and will provide more opportunities.

For example, consider the job Computer Software Engineers, Systems Software, which is expected to grow by 43.0% between 2004 and 2014. Overall, opportunities will be good for these workers, but when you look at specific fields you discover a lot of variation in outlook. Employment in the field of Software Publishers is expected to grow at the stunning rate of 91.8%, whereas employment in Telecommunications is actually expected to *shrink* by 6.7%. So you can see how knowing facts like this can help your job-hunting strategies and possibly your decisions about your education. That's why in chapter 5, where each of the 100 hot jobs is described, we include a list of the fields that offer the most growth for each job.

The present chapter provides an overview of the hottest fields that are employing workers in the 100 hot job targets. The classification of fields we use here is based on the Department of Labor publication *Career Guide to Industries* and is also used in *40 Best Fields for Your Career* (JIST).

The 10 Hottest Fields Employing the 100 Hot Job Targets

These are the 10 fields that will have the largest increases in employment of workers in the 100 hot job targets between 2004 and 2014. (This is the most recent period of time for which projections are available, and the trends of growth projected for that time period probably will not change much for several years beyond that.) To identify them, we looked at two measures of employment growth—absolute numbers and percentages—and chose the 10 fields with the best combination.

Field	Increase in Employment of the 100 Hot Jobs	Percent Growth of the 100 Hot Jobs
1. Employment Services	881,066	49.3%
2. Computer Systems Design and Related Services	320,308	49.1%
3. Health Care	2,140,240	29.0%
4. Management, Scientific, and Technical Consulting Services	208,797	64.5%
5. Child Day Care Services	166,291	40.5%
6. Educational Services	1,426,024	19.6%
7. Software Publishers	105,111	77.9%
8. Social Assistance, Except Child Day Care	153,404	32.3%
9. Arts, Entertainment, and Recreation	142,709	23.9%
10. Internet Service Providers, Web Search Portals, and Data Processing Services	76,060	38.4%

Following are descriptions of these 10 fields, based on information from the U.S. Department of Labor.

1. Employment Services

	All Jobs in This Field	The 100 Hot Jobs in This Field
• Average Annual Earnings	$22,160	$27,081
• Average Job Growth	45.5%	49.3%
• Size of Workforce	3,501,880	1,788,172

Significant Points

- Employment services ranks among the fields projected to grow the fastest and to provide the most new jobs.

- Most temporary jobs in this field require only graduation from high school, while some permanent jobs may require a bachelor's or higher degree.

- Temporary jobs provide an entry into the workforce, supplemental income, and a bridge to full-time employment for many workers.

Nature of the Field

Although many people associate the employment services field with temporary employment opportunities for clerical workers, the field matches millions of people with jobs, providing both temporary and permanent employment to individuals with a wide variety of education and managerial and professional work experience. Occupations in the field range from secretary to computer systems analyst and from general laborer to nurse. In addition to temporary jobs in these occupations, permanent positions in the field include workers such as employment interviewers and marketing representatives who help assign and place workers in jobs.

Outlook

Most new jobs will arise in the largest occupational groups in this industry—office and administrative support, production, and transportation and material moving occupations. However, the continuing trend toward specialization also will spur growth among professional workers, including engineers, computer specialists, and health care practitioners such as registered nurses. Managers also will see an increase in new jobs as government increasingly contracts out management functions. In addition, growth of temporary help firms and professional employer organizations—which provide human resource management, risk management, accounting, and information technology services—will provide more opportunities for professional workers within those fields. Marketing and sales representative jobs in temporary staffing firms also are expected to increase, and competition is expected to heat up among these firms for the most qualified workers and the best clients.

Fastest-Growing Hot Jobs in This Field

Job	Percent Growth in This Field Through 2014
1. Customer Service Representatives	74.4%
2. Construction Laborers	66.7%
3. Registered Nurses	50.5%
4. Office Clerks, General	49.3%
5. Helpers—Production Workers	35.0%
6. Laborers and Freight, Stock, and Material Movers, Hand	34.7%

2. Computer Systems Design and Related Services

	All Jobs in This Field	The 100 Hot Jobs in This Field
• Average Annual Earnings	$63,600	$60,873
• Average Job Growth	39.5%	49.1%
• Size of Workforce	1,149,800	652,852

Significant Points

- The computer systems design and related services field is expected to experience rapid growth, adding 453,000 jobs between 2004 and 2014.

- Professional and related workers enjoy the best prospects, reflecting continuing demand for higher-level skills needed to keep up with changes in technology.

- Computer specialists account for 53 percent of all employees in this field.

Nature of the Field

All organizations today rely on computer and information technology to conduct business and operate more efficiently. Often, however, these institutions do not have the internal resources to implement new technologies effectively or satisfy their changing needs. When faced with these limitations, organizations turn to the computer systems design and related services field to meet their specialized needs on a contract or customer basis.

> According to the Information Technology Association of America, 92% of all information technology (IT) workers are in companies in fields other than IT, and 80% of these are small companies.

Outlook

An increasing reliance on information technology, combined with falling prices of computers and related hardware, means that individuals and organizations will continue to turn to computer systems design and related services firms to maximize the return on their investments in equipment and to fulfill their growing computing needs. Job opportunities will be favorable for most workers. However, employment growth will not be as robust as it was during the last decade due to increasing productivity and offshore outsourcing of some job functions to lower-wage foreign countries.

Fastest-Growing Hot Jobs in This Field

Job	Percent Growth in This Field Through 2014
1. Network Systems and Data Communications Analysts	81.5%
2. Computer Software Engineers, Applications	62.7%
3. Computer Software Engineers, Systems Software	62.2%
4. Computer Security Specialists	58.1%
5. Computer Systems Analysts	49.2%
6. Customer Service Representatives	40.6%
7. Computer Support Specialists	35.6%
8. Office Clerks, General	20.7%

3. Health Care

	All Jobs in This Field	The 100 Hot Jobs in This Field
• Average Annual Earnings	$32,681	$37,585
• Average Job Growth	27.3%	29.0%
• Size of Workforce	13,062,102	7,373,104

Significant Points

- In addition to 13 million jobs for wage and salary workers, health care provided about 411,000 jobs for the self-employed.

- 8 out of the 20 occupations projected to grow the fastest are in health care.

- More new wage and salary jobs created through 2014 will be in health care than in any other field—about 19 percent, or 3.6 million.

- Most workers have jobs that require less than 4 years of college education, but health diagnosing and treating practitioners are among the most educated workers.

Nature of the Field

Combining medical technology and the human touch, the health care field administers care around the clock, responding to the needs of millions of people—from newborns to the critically ill.

Health care is one of the high-growth fields that the U.S. Department of Labor has targeted for special attention. It is growing so fast that the Department of Labor is working with representatives of industry and education to try to prevent shortages of workers.

Outlook

Job opportunities should be excellent in all employment settings because of high job turnover, particularly from the large number of expected retirements and tougher immigration rules that are slowing the numbers of foreign health care workers entering the U.S.

Fastest-Growing Hot Jobs in This Field

Job	Percent Growth in This Field Through 2014
1. Medical Assistants	53.7%
2. Receptionists and Information Clerks	31.3%
3. Registered Nurses	30.5%
4. Nursing Aides, Orderlies, and Attendants	22.2%
5. Office Clerks, General	16.8%

4. Management, Scientific, and Technical Consulting Services

	All Jobs in This Field	The 100 Hot Jobs in This Field
• Average Annual Earnings	$47,310	$44,665
• Average Job Growth	60.5%	64.5%
• Size of Workforce	794,520	323,867

Significant Points

- This field ranks among the fastest growing through the year 2014; however, job competition should remain keen, with the most educated and experienced workers having the best job prospects.
- This field is one of the highest paying.
- About 25 percent of all workers are self-employed.
- About 72 percent of workers have a bachelor's or higher degree; 59 percent of all jobs are in managerial, business, financial, and professional occupations.

Nature of the Field

Management, scientific, and technical consulting firms influence how businesses, governments, and institutions make decisions. Often working behind the scenes, these firms offer resources that clients cannot provide themselves. Usually, one of the resources is expertise—in the form of knowledge, experience, special skills, or creativity; another resource is time or personnel that the client cannot spare.

> Consulting offers many opportunities for self-employment. You may establish your expertise while working for a consulting company and later set up your own business to market your skills. However, note that many of the fastest-growing jobs in this field provide clerical and administrative *support* for consultants.

Outlook

All areas of consulting should experience strong growth. Still, despite the projected growth in the industry, job competition should remain keen because the prestigious and independent nature of the work and the generous salary and benefits attract more job seekers than openings every year. Because of the high degree of competition, those with the most education and job experience will likely have the best prospects.

Fastest-Growing Hot Jobs in This Field

Job	Percent Growth in This Field Through 2014
1. Customer Service Representatives	69.6%
2. Employment Interviewers	65.6%
3. Personnel Recruiters	65.6%
4. Bookkeeping, Accounting, and Auditing Clerks	49.6%
5. Executive Secretaries and Administrative Assistants	48.9%
6. Office Clerks, General	48.0%

5. Child Day Care Services

	All Jobs in This Field	The 100 Hot Jobs in This Field
• Average Annual Earnings	$18,510	$20,523
• Average Job Growth	38.4%	40.5%
• Size of Workforce	734,400	410,376

Significant Points

- Preschool teachers, teacher assistants, and child care workers account for about 3 out of 4 wage and salary jobs.

- About 45 percent of all child day care workers have a high school degree or less, reflecting the minimal training requirements for most jobs.

- More than a quarter of all employees work part time, and nearly 3 out of 10 full-time employees in the field work more than 40 hours per week.

- Job openings should be numerous because dissatisfaction with benefits, pay, and stressful working conditions causes many to leave the field.

Nature of the Field

Obtaining affordable, quality child day care, especially for children under age 5, is a major concern for many parents. With the increasing number of households in which both parents work full time, this field has been one of the fastest growing in the U.S. economy. The field consists of establishments that provide paid care for infants, toddlers, preschool children, or older children in before- and after-school programs.

Although this field tends not to pay high wages, it is growing very rapidly. It also can give great personal satisfaction from helping other people and touching young lives.

Outlook

Center-based care should continue to expand its share of the field because an increasing number of parents prefer its more formal setting and believe that it provides a better foundation for children before they begin traditional schooling. However, some parents prefer the more personal attention their children get from family child care providers, so this part of the field will continue to remain an important source of care for many young children.

Fastest-Growing Hot Jobs in This Field

Job	Percent Growth in This Field Through 2014
1. Preschool Teachers, Except Special Education	41.2%
2. Teacher Assistants	41.2%

6. Educational Services

	All Jobs in This Field	The 100 Hot Jobs in This Field
• Average Annual Earnings	$36,860	$36,411
• Average Job Growth	16.6%	19.6%
• Size of Workforce	12,778,104	7,371,752

Significant Points

- With about 1 in 4 Americans enrolled in educational institutions, educational services is the second largest field, accounting for about 13.0 million jobs (including the self-employed).

- Most teaching positions—which constitute almost half of all educational services jobs—require at least a bachelor's degree, and some require a master's or doctoral degree.

- Retirements in a number of education professions will create many job openings.

Nature of the Field

The education people get is a major influence on both the types of jobs they are able to hold and their earnings. Lifelong learning is important in acquiring new knowledge and upgrading one's skills, particularly in this age of rapid technological and economic changes. The educational services field includes a variety of institutions that offer academic education, vocational or career and technical instruction, and other education and training to millions of students each year.

Jobs in this field tend to have more security than average.

Outlook

Over the long term, the overall demand for workers in educational services will increase as a result of a growing emphasis on improving education and making it available not only to more children and young adults, but also to those currently employed but in need of improving their skills. Reforms, such as universal preschool and all-day kindergarten, will require more preschool and kindergarten teachers. However, low enrollment growth projections at the elementary, middle, and secondary school level are likely to slow growth somewhat, resulting in average growth for these teachers.

Fastest-Growing Hot Jobs in This Field

Job	Percent Growth in This Field Through 2014
1. Vocational Education Teachers, Postsecondary	32.7%
2. Elementary School Teachers, Except Special Education	17.9%
3. Secondary School Teachers, Except Special and Vocational Education	14.3%
4. Teacher Assistants	10.9%
5. Office Clerks, General	8.1%

15

7. Software Publishers

	All Jobs in This Field	The 100 Hot Jobs in This Field
• Average Annual Earnings	$71,040	$66,381
• Average Job Growth	67.6%	77.9%
• Size of Workforce	235,130	135,011

Significant Points

- Employment is projected to increase 68 percent between 2004 and 2014, ranking software publishers as the third-fastest-growing field in the economy.

- Computer specialists account for 52 percent of all workers.

- Job opportunities will be excellent for most workers; professional workers enjoy the best prospects, reflecting continuing demand for higher-level skills needed to keep up with changes in technology.

Together with computer systems design and related services and with Internet service providers, Web search portals, and data processing services, software publishers is part of the larger field of information technology, another one of the high-growth fields that the U.S. Department of Labor has identified.

Nature of the Field

Computer software is needed to run and protect computer systems and networks. Software publishing establishments carry out the functions necessary for producing and distributing computer software, such as designing, providing documentation, assisting in installation, and providing support services to software purchasers.

Outlook

Given the increasingly widespread use of information technologies and the overall rate of growth expected for the software publishing industry, most occupations should grow very rapidly, although some will grow faster than others. The most rapid job increases will occur among computer specialists such as computer software engineers as firms continue to install sophisticated computer networks, set up Internet and intranet sites, and engage in electronic commerce and as consumers continue to explore and use vast amounts of applications software.

Fastest-Growing Hot Jobs in This Field

Job	Percent Growth in This Field Through 2014
1. Computer Software Engineers, Applications	93.0%
2. Computer Software Engineers, Systems Software	91.8%
3. Computer Systems Analysts	76.9%
4. Customer Service Representatives	64.7%
5. Computer Support Specialists	60.8%

8. Social Assistance, Except Child Day Care

	All Jobs in This Field	The 100 Hot Jobs in This Field
● Average Annual Earnings	$23,172	$28,847
● Average Job Growth	32.6%	32.3%
● Size of Workforce	1,305,420	475,274

Significant Points

- About 1 out of 3 jobs are in professional and service occupations.
- Job opportunities in social assistance should be numerous through the year 2014 because of job turnover and rapid employment growth.
- Some of the fastest-growing occupations in the nation, such as home health aides and personal and home care aides, are concentrated in social assistance.
- Average earnings are low because of the large number of part-time and low-paying service jobs.

Some of the fastest-growing occupations in this field are not included in this book because their average pay is too low. The field continues to attract workers who enjoy helping other people and who want the security of a field with lots of job openings.

Nature of the Field

Careers in social assistance appeal to persons with a strong desire to make life better and easier for others. Workers in this field usually are good communicators and enjoy interacting with people. Social assistance establishments provide a wide array of services that include helping the homeless, counseling troubled and emotionally disturbed individuals, training the unemployed or underemployed, and helping the needy to obtain financial assistance.

Outlook

Projected job growth is due mostly to the expansion of services for the elderly and the aging baby-boom generation. Similarly, services for the mentally ill, the physically disabled, and families in crisis will be expanded. Increasing emphasis on providing home care services rather than more costly nursing home or hospital care and on earlier and better integration of the physically disabled and mentally ill into society also will contribute to employment growth in the social assistance field, as will increased demand for drug and alcohol abuse prevention programs.

Fastest-Growing Hot Jobs in This Field

Job	Percent Growth in This Field Through 2014
1. Social and Human Service Assistants	45.6%
2. Social and Community Service Managers	32.5%
3. Office Clerks, General	18.1%

9. Arts, Entertainment, and Recreation

	All Jobs in This Field	The 100 Hot Jobs in This Field
• Average Annual Earnings	$20,540	$26,262
• Average Job Growth	25.1%	23.9%
• Size of Workforce	1,842,820	596,042

Significant Points

- The field is characterized by a large number of seasonal and part-time jobs and relatively young workers.
- About 40 percent of all workers have no formal education beyond high school.
- Rising incomes, more leisure time, and growing awareness of the health benefits of physical fitness will increase the demand for arts, entertainment, and recreation services.
- Earnings are relatively low.

Some jobs in the arts are missing from this book because income information is unavailable. But most are absent because opportunities are limited or income is low.

Nature of the Field

As leisure time and personal incomes have grown across the nation, so has the arts, entertainment, and recreation field. Practically any activity that occupies a person's leisure time, excluding the viewing of motion pictures and video rentals, is part of this field. The diverse range of activities offered by this field can be categorized into three broad groups—live performances or events; historical, cultural, or educational exhibits; and recreation or leisure-time activities.

Outlook

The arts, entertainment, and recreation field has relied heavily on workers under the age of 25 to fill seasonal and unskilled positions. About one-fourth of all jobs in this field are held by workers under age 25, compared to 14 percent in all fields combined. Opportunities should be available for young, seasonal, part-time, and unskilled workers. In addition, the field is expected to hire a growing number of workers in other age groups.

Fastest-Growing Hot Jobs in This Field

Job	Percent Growth in This Field Through 2014
1. Fitness Trainers and Aerobics Instructors	28.7%
2. Landscaping and Groundskeeping Workers	24.5%
3. Receptionists and Information Clerks	22.6%
4. Security Guards	4.3%

10. Internet Service Providers, Web Search Portals, and Data Processing Services

	All Jobs in This Field	The 100 Hot Jobs in This Field
• Average Annual Earnings	$48,070	$50,438
• Average Job Growth	27.8%	38.4%
• Size of Workforce	383,540	197,940

Significant Points

- Projected employment growth varies by field sector, but all segments should grow faster than the economy as a whole.
- About a third of all jobs are in computer occupations; another third are in office and administrative support occupations.
- About 2 out of 5 jobs are in California, Texas, Florida, Virginia, and New York.

Outlook

In Internet service providers and Web search portals, job opportunities should be best for computer specialists, such as computer software engineers and network systems and data communications analysts. There should be strong continuing demand for these and other computer specialists to maintain and upgrade the systems that keep users connected and the search engines that make the Web navigable. As companies in this field continue to add services and content, they will need these workers to implement the changes. Demand for computer specialists also should experience solid growth in data processing, hosting, and related services, particularly in Web hosting services.

Fastest-Growing Hot Jobs in This Field

Job	Percent Growth in This Field Through 2014
1. Network Systems and Data Communications Analysts	69.2%
2. Computer Software Engineers, Systems Software	56.5%
3. Computer Software Engineers, Applications	56.3%
4. Computer Security Specialists	50.4%
5. Computer Systems Analysts	47.6%
6. Customer Service Representatives	31.5%
7. Computer Support Specialists	27.9%
8. Office Clerks, General	20.3%
9. First-Line Supervisors/Managers of Office and Administrative Support Workers	20.0%
10. Bookkeeping, Accounting, and Auditing Clerks	19.0%

Key Points: Chapter 2

- For smart career planning, it helps to know not only the hot job targets, but also the hot fields.
- Some fields are growing extremely fast but are still small (for example, software publishers), whereas others are not growing quite as fast but are so large that they will create numerous job openings (for example, health care).

Chapter 3

Where the Jobs Are Now: Metropolitan Areas with Fast Workforce Growth and Low Unemployment

Some parts of the United States are growing much faster than others. If you are planning your career, you may want to relocate to an area where the workforce has been expanding most rapidly and where unemployment is low.

In this chapter you'll see profiles of the hottest metropolitan areas and tips on what to consider before pulling up stakes and moving.

The 10 Hottest Metropolitan Areas

We looked at the statistics for all the metropolitan areas to see which gained the biggest percentages of wage-earning workers in recent years. Note that we were not looking at growth of the total *population*, which includes children, retirees, and others who are not working; we also were not looking at growth of self-employed workers. We excluded any metropolitan area with more than 6.5% percent unemployment. The resulting list therefore indicates where economic growth is particularly hot.

These are the 10 metropolitan areas that recently experienced both rapid workforce growth and low unemployment. The fastest-growing are listed closest to the top.

Metropolitan Area	Percent Growth of Wage-Earning Workforce	Unemployment
1. Cape Coral–Fort Myers, FL	7.9%	5.4%
2. Orlando–Kissimmee, FL	7.1%	6.2%
3. Medford, OR	6.3%	5.7%
4. Lakeland, FL	5.9%	5.1%
5. Sheboygan, WI	5.7%	6.0%
6. Savannah, GA	5.6%	6.1%
7. Phoenix–Mesa–Scottsdale, AZ	5.6%	5.5%
8. St. Cloud, MN	4.8%	4.2%
9. La Crosse, WI–MN	4.7%	5.2%
10. Bellingham, WA	4.5%	5.4%

Figures on percent of workforce growth are based on the years 2004–2005; figures on unemployment are based on 2005. These are the most recent figures that were available.

Following are profiles of these 10 hot metropolitan areas, based on information from the U.S. Census Bureau. The order of occupational groups and fields in the following charts is based on the classification scheme used by the U.S. Department of Labor.

1. Cape Coral–Fort Myers, FL

- Civilian labor force: 253,076
- Employment of men: 95.1%
- Employment of women: 93.9%
- Unemployed: 5.4%
- Median household income: $46,053

Major Occupational Groups Employing Civilian Workers

Occupational Group	Percent of Workers Employed
Management, professional, and related	25.6%
Service	16.8%
Sales and office	27.3%
Farming, fishing, and forestry	0.8%
Construction, extraction, maintenance, and repair	16.4%
Production, transportation, and material-moving	7.7%

Major Fields Employing Civilian Workers

Field	Percent of Workers Employed
Agriculture, forestry, fishing, hunting, and mining	0.9%
Construction	17.0%
Manufacturing	4.0%
Wholesale trade	3.3%
Retail trade	13.1%
Transportation, warehousing, and utilities	3.4%
Information	2.0%
Finance, insurance, and real estate	7.8%
Professional, scientific, and managerial services	9.2%
Educational services, health care, and social assistance	15.6%
Arts, entertainment, recreation, accommodation, and food services	10.7%
Other services, except public administration	3.9%
Public administration	3.6%

2. Orlando–Kissimmee, FL

- Civilian labor force: 990,766
- Employment of men: 94.4%
- Employment of women: 92.9%
- Unemployed: 6.2%
- Median household income: $44,543

Major Occupational Groups Employing Civilian Workers	
Occupational Group	Percent of Workers Employed
Management, professional, and related	30.5%
Service	17.5%
Sales and office	26.7%
Farming, fishing, and forestry	0.4%
Construction, extraction, maintenance, and repair	10.4%
Production, transportation, and material-moving	8.3%

Major Fields Employing Civilian Workers	
Field	Percent of Workers Employed
Agriculture, forestry, fishing, hunting, and mining	0.5%
Construction	9.2%
Manufacturing	4.8%
Wholesale trade	3.7%
Retail trade	11.3%
Transportation, warehousing, and utilities	4.6%
Information	3.1%
Finance, insurance, and real estate	7.7%
Professional, scientific, and managerial services	12.3%
Educational services, health care, and social assistance	14.8%
Arts, entertainment, recreation, accommodation, and food services	14.5%
Other services, except public administration	4.4%
Public administration	2.7%

3. Medford, OR

- Civilian labor force: 98,578
- Employment of men: 95.2%
- Employment of women: 93.4%
- Unemployed: 5.7%
- Median household income: $41,194

Major Occupational Groups Employing Civilian Workers	
Occupational Group	Percent of Workers Employed
Management, professional, and related	26.3%
Service	15.4%
Sales and office	24.4%
Farming, fishing, and forestry	1.2%
Construction, extraction, maintenance, and repair	11.1%
Production, transportation, and material-moving	15.9%

Major Fields Employing Civilian Workers	
Field	Percent of Workers Employed
Agriculture, forestry, fishing, hunting, and mining	2.5%
Construction	9.0%
Manufacturing	9.6%
Wholesale trade	2.7%
Retail trade	15.9%
Transportation, warehousing, and utilities	3.4%
Information	1.2%
Finance, insurance, and real estate	6.9%
Professional, scientific, and managerial services	7.4%
Educational services, health care, and social assistance	18.1%
Arts, entertainment, recreation, accommodation, and food services	8.8%
Other services, except public administration	4.4%
Public administration	4.4%

4. Lakeland, FL

- Civilian labor force: 245,423
- Employment of men: 95.4%
- Employment of women: 94.3%
- Unemployed: 5.1%
- Median household income: $39,124

Major Occupational Groups Employing Civilian Workers	
Occupational Group	Percent of Workers Employed
Management, professional, and related	26.0%
Service	15.4%
Sales and office	26.0%
Farming, fishing, and forestry	0.7%
Construction, extraction, maintenance, and repair	12.0%
Production, transportation, and material-moving	14.9%

Major Fields Employing Civilian Workers	
Field	Percent of Workers Employed
Agriculture, forestry, fishing, hunting, and mining	2.2%
Construction	9.9%
Manufacturing	6.8%
Wholesale trade	3.5%
Retail trade	13.9%
Transportation, warehousing, and utilities	5.9%
Information	1.8%
Finance, insurance, and real estate	6.4%
Professional, scientific, and managerial services	9.4%
Educational services, health care, and social assistance	16.3%
Arts, entertainment, recreation, accommodation, and food services	10.3%
Other services, except public administration	5.1%
Public administration	3.3%

5. Sheboygan, WI

- Civilian labor force: 63,448
- Employment of men: 93.4%
- Employment of women: 94.7%
- Unemployed: 6.0%
- Median household income: $51,034

Major Occupational Groups Employing Civilian Workers	
Occupational Group	Percent of Workers Employed
Management, professional, and related	26.2%
Service	14.4%
Sales and office	21.7%
Farming, fishing, and forestry	0.6%
Construction, extraction, maintenance, and repair	7.4%
Production, transportation, and material-moving	23.7%

Major Fields Employing Civilian Workers	
Field	Percent of Workers Employed
Agriculture, forestry, fishing, hunting, and mining	2.0%
Construction	4.6%
Manufacturing	33.0%
Wholesale trade	3.7%
Retail trade	9.8%
Transportation, warehousing, and utilities	2.2%
Information	0.8%
Finance, insurance, and real estate	4.2%
Professional, scientific, and managerial services	6.1%
Educational services, health care, and social assistance	15.2%
Arts, entertainment, recreation, accommodation, and food services	6.9%
Other services, except public administration	3.0%
Public administration	2.3%

6. Savannah, GA

- Civilian labor force: 152,456
- Employment of men: 94.2%
- Employment of women: 93.5%
- Unemployed: 6.1%
- Median household income: $46,240

Major Occupational Groups Employing Civilian Workers	
Occupational Group	Percent of Workers Employed
Management, professional, and related	29.6%
Service	15.3%
Sales and office	24.9%
Farming, fishing, and forestry	0.3%
Construction, extraction, maintenance, and repair	10.1%
Production, transportation, and material-moving	13.8%

Major Fields Employing Civilian Workers	
Field	Percent of Workers Employed
Agriculture, forestry, fishing, hunting, and mining	0.6%
Construction	7.9%
Manufacturing	8.9%
Wholesale trade	3.2%
Retail trade	10.7%
Transportation, warehousing, and utilities	8.5%
Information	1.3%
Finance, insurance, and real estate	5.6%
Professional, scientific, and managerial services	7.4%
Educational services, health care, and social assistance	20.4%
Arts, entertainment, recreation, accommodation, and food services	8.7%
Other services, except public administration	5.3%
Public administration	5.3%

7. Phoenix–Mesa–Scottsdale, AZ

- Civilian labor force: 1,896,329
- Employment of men: 94.8%
- Employment of women: 94.1%
- Unemployed: 5.5%
- Median household income: $48,124

Major Occupational Groups Employing Civilian Workers	
Occupational Group	Percent of Workers Employed
Management, professional, and related	31.6%
Service	15.4%
Sales and office	26.2%
Farming, fishing, and forestry	0.4%
Construction, extraction, maintenance, and repair	11.0%
Production, transportation, and material-moving	9.9%

Major Fields Employing Civilian Workers	
Field	Percent of Workers Employed
Agriculture, forestry, fishing, hunting, and mining	0.7%
Construction	10.1%
Manufacturing	8.5%
Wholesale trade	3.5%
Retail trade	11.4%
Transportation, warehousing, and utilities	4.4%
Information	2.0%
Finance, insurance, and real estate	9.6%
Professional, scientific, and managerial services	11.0%
Educational services, health care, and social assistance	16.3%
Arts, entertainment, recreation, accommodation, and food services	8.8%
Other services, except public administration	4.1%
Public administration	4.2%

8. St. Cloud, MN

- Civilian labor force: 103,533
- Employment of men: 95.6%
- Employment of women: 96.0%
- Unemployed: 4.2%
- Median household income: $46,367

Major Occupational Groups Employing Civilian Workers	
Occupational Group	Percent of Workers Employed
Management, professional, and related	26.3%
Service	14.6%
Sales and office	25.9%
Farming, fishing, and forestry	0.7%
Construction, extraction, maintenance, and repair	10.8%
Production, transportation, and material-moving	17.5%

Major Fields Employing Civilian Workers	
Field	Percent of Workers Employed
Agriculture, forestry, fishing, hunting, and mining	3.4%
Construction	8.5%
Manufacturing	16.8%
Wholesale trade	3.6%
Retail trade	13.8%
Transportation, warehousing, and utilities	3.6%
Information	1.2%
Finance, insurance, and real estate	4.6%
Professional, scientific, and managerial services	6.4%
Educational services, health care, and social assistance	20.3%
Arts, entertainment, recreation, accommodation, and food services	6.8%
Other services, except public administration	4.2%
Public administration	2.8%

9. La Crosse, WI–MN

- Civilian labor force: 70,717
- Employment of men: 93.1%
- Employment of women: 96.5%
- Unemployed: 5.2%
- Median household income: $45,155

Major Occupational Groups Employing Civilian Workers	
Occupational Group	Percent of Workers Employed
Management, professional, and related	32.2%
Service	16.7%
Sales and office	24.9%
Farming, fishing, and forestry	0.5%
Construction, extraction, maintenance, and repair	8.3%
Production, transportation, and material-moving	12.2%

Major Fields Employing Civilian Workers	
Field	Percent of Workers Employed
Agriculture, forestry, fishing, hunting, and mining	1.9%
Construction	5.9%
Manufacturing	13.5%
Wholesale trade	2.8%
Retail trade	15.4%
Transportation, warehousing, and utilities	3.2%
Information	3.2%
Finance, insurance, and real estate	5.0%
Professional, scientific, and managerial services	5.7%
Educational services, health care, and social assistance	24.8%
Arts, entertainment, recreation, accommodation, and food services	8.1%
Other services, except public administration	3.2%
Public administration	2.3%

10. Bellingham, WA

- Civilian labor force: 96,172
- Employment of men: 93.8%
- Employment of women: 95.6%
- Unemployed: 5.4%
- Median household income: $44,248

Major Occupational Groups Employing Civilian Workers	
Occupational Group	Percent of Workers Employed
Management, professional, and related	29.8%
Service	16.7%
Sales and office	26.2%
Farming, fishing, and forestry	1.6%
Construction, extraction, maintenance, and repair	9.2%
Production, transportation, and material-moving	11.1%

Major Fields Employing Civilian Workers	
Field	Percent of Workers Employed
Agriculture, forestry, fishing, hunting, and mining	3.0%
Construction	6.7%
Manufacturing	10.7%
Wholesale trade	3.1%
Retail trade	12.3%
Transportation, warehousing, and utilities	3.6%
Information	2.8%
Finance, insurance, and real estate	5.5%
Professional, scientific, and managerial services	6.5%
Educational services, health care, and social assistance	20.4%
Arts, entertainment, recreation, accommodation, and food services	11.2%
Other services, except public administration	5.0%
Public administration	3.9%

What to Consider Before Relocating

Here are some considerations to bear in mind before you relocate to find better chances of landing a job:

- **Continued growth.** The metropolitan areas profiled in this chapter were chosen because of recent growth and low unemployment. However, there are no guarantees that these areas will continue to grow at this pace or maintain the same low level of unemployment. Before moving to another area, you should investigate whether local economic trends are expected to remain favorable. You may be able to find projections of job openings at the Web site of the state department of labor or office of employment security. The appendix identifies a site with links to these state departments.

- **Opportunities in your field.** The 10 hottest metropolitan areas were chosen on the basis of their *overall* economic performance. For the particular career goal you have in mind, they may not be the most promising places to hunt for a job. The appendix identifies a site that lets you choose an occupation and compare its wages and employment trends across states and communities.

- **Networking.** Your network of contacts is probably concentrated in the area where you live now. If you move to a new area where you don't know anyone, you'll lose an important advantage in job hunting. If possible, choose an area where you know at least a few people—either directly or through your network. Also, investigate whether your targeted area offers opportunities for you to network quickly. Perhaps there are local branches of a social, religious, or hobby-centered organization to which you now belong or where you would fit in readily.

- **Your resume.** In a new location, your resume may not carry as much clout as it does where you live now. Employers in other regions may not be familiar with your previous employers or the school or college you attended. Try to find out from the job-placement office of your school or college whether graduates have found jobs in the area you are targeting. Of course, if you have training from the armed forces or a nationally registered apprenticeship program or if you have education from a college with a national reputation, this is not a concern. This is also less of an issue if you are aiming for an occupation in which on-the-job training is the usual entry route.

- **Culture shock.** Every region of the United States has its own unique culture, so before you move you should visit your planned destination and make sure you feel comfortable there. Will you fit in with the people who live there? Will you find enjoyable leisure activities? Even the weather patterns may affect your level of comfort. Of course, it is possible that you don't fit in well where you are now and would enjoy a change of scene.

Given these concerns, the ideal strategy for relocating to find work would be to get hired for a job in the new location *before* you move—but this can be very difficult to do. A compromise strategy would be to set up temporary, bare-bones living quarters in the new location, find employment there, and then settle into your new location.

Key Points: Chapter 3

- It may be easier to find work in a city or town where the economy is booming. With research, you may be able to identify the places with the best opportunities for your career goal.

- In the location where you now live, you probably have a better network of contacts, a resume that is more effective with employers, and a better familiarity with the culture than you would have in a distant location. Nevertheless, depending on your career goal and where you live now, your best chances of finding work may be in another city or town.

Chapter 4

Match Yourself to Hot Careers

With 100 hot job targets to choose from, you probably would appreciate some help with narrowing down your options. That's what this chapter is for. In the following pages you're going to gain some insights into the work-related aspects of your personality and learn which of the 100 hot careers best suit your personality. Of course, personality is not the only factor you should consider when you make a career choice. But it's a good place to start because it provides a big-picture view of the world of work.

The most widely used personality theory about careers was developed by John L. Holland in the early 1950s. The theory rests on the principle that people tend to be happier and more successful in jobs where they feel comfortable with the work tasks and problems, the physical environment, and the kinds of people who are co-workers. Holland identified six personality types that describe basic aspects of work situations. He called them Realistic, Investigative, Artistic, Social, Enterprising, and Conventional. (Some of these labels are difficult to grasp at first glance, but you'll gain a clearer understanding by the time you finish this chapter.) The initials for these personality types spell RIASEC, so that is often used to refer to these types.

Holland argued that most people can be described by one of the RIASEC personality types—the type that dominates—and that likewise each of the various occupations that make up our economy can be described as having work situations and settings compatible with one of these personality types. Therefore, if you understand your dominant personality type and then identify which jobs are consistent with that type, you will have a clearer idea of which jobs will suit you best.

Holland recognized that many people and jobs also tend toward a second or third personality type—for example, someone might be described primarily as Social and secondarily as Enterprising, and such a person would fit in best working in a job with the "SE" code, such as Social and

Community Service Managers. People like this should also consider jobs coded "ES," such as Personnel Recruiters, and they might find satisfaction in many jobs with a variety of Holland codes beginning with either S or E.

Next you're going to do a quick exercise to help you clarify your main personality type or types. Keep in mind that personality measurement is not an exact science and this fast checklist is not a scientific instrument. Nevertheless, it should give you insights that will help you understand which kinds of work suit you best. Use common sense to combine the results of this exercise with other information you can get about yourself and your work options. Talk to people who know you and are familiar with your school and work experiences.

The exercise is easy to do—just follow the directions beginning with Step 1. This is not a test, so there are no right or wrong answers and no time limit.

If someone else will be using this book, you should photocopy the following six pages and mark your responses on the photocopy.

Step 1: Respond to the Statements

Starting on the next page, carefully read each work activity (items 1 through 120). If you think you would LIKE to do the activity, circle the number of the activity. Don't consider whether you have the education or training needed for it or how much money you might earn if it were part of your job. Simply decide whether you would like the activity. If you know you would dislike the activity or you're not sure, leave the number unmarked.

After you respond to all 120 activities, you'll score your responses in Step 2.

Circle the numbers of the activities you would LIKE to do.

1. Build kitchen cabinets

2. Guard money in an armored car

3. Operate a dairy farm

4. Lay brick or tile

5. Monitor a machine on an assembly line

6. Repair household appliances

7. Drive a taxicab

8. Assemble electronic parts

9. Drive a truck to deliver packages to offices and homes

10. Paint houses

11. Enforce fish and game laws

12. Work on an offshore oil-drilling rig

13. Perform lawn care services

14. Catch fish as a member of a fishing crew

15. Refinish furniture

16. Fix a broken faucet

17. Do cleaning or maintenance work

18. Test the quality of parts before shipment

19. Operate a motorboat to carry passengers

20. Put out forest fires

____ **Page Score for R**

(continued)

(continued)

Circle the numbers of the activities you would LIKE to do.

21. Study the history of past civilizations

22. Study animal behavior

23. Develop a new medicine

24. Study ways to reduce water pollution

25. Determine the infection rate of a new disease

26. Study rocks and minerals

27. Diagnose and treat sick animals

28. Study the personalities of world leaders

29. Study whales and other types of marine life

30. Investigate crimes

31. Study the movement of planets

32. Examine blood samples using a microscope

33. Investigate the cause of a fire

34. Develop psychological profiles of criminals

35. Invent a replacement for sugar

36. Study genetics

37. Study the governments of different countries

38. Do research on plants or animals

39. Do laboratory tests to identify diseases

40. Study weather conditions

____ **Page Score for I**

Circle the numbers of the activities you would LIKE to do.

41. Direct a play

42. Create dance routines for a show

43. Write books or plays

44. Play a musical instrument

45. Write reviews of books or plays

46. Compose or arrange music

47. Act in a movie

48. Dance in a Broadway show

49. Draw pictures

50. Create special effects for movies

51. Conduct a musical choir

52. Audition singers and musicians for a musical show

53. Design sets for plays

54. Announce a radio show

55. Write a song

56. Perform jazz or tap dance

57. Direct a movie

58. Sing in a band

59. Design artwork for magazines

60. Pose for a photographer

____ **Page Score for A**

(continued)

(continued)

Circle the numbers of the activities you would LIKE to do.

61. Perform nursing duties in a hospital

62. Give CPR to someone who has stopped breathing

63. Help people with personal or emotional problems

64. Teach children how to read

65. Work with mentally disabled children

66. Teach an elementary school class

67. Give career guidance to people

68. Supervise the activities of children at a camp

69. Help people with family-related problems

70. Perform rehabilitation therapy

71. Help elderly people with their daily activities

72. Teach children how to play sports

73. Teach sign language to people with hearing disabilities

74. Help people who have problems with drugs or alcohol

75. Help families care for ill relatives

76. Provide massage therapy to people

77. Plan exercises for disabled students

78. Organize activities at a recreational facility

79. Take care of children at a day-care center

80. Teach a high school class

____ **Page Score for S**

Circle the numbers of the activities you would LIKE to do.

81. Buy and sell stocks and bonds

82. Manage a retail store

83. Operate a beauty salon or barbershop

84. Sell merchandise over the telephone

85. Run a stand that sells newspapers and magazines

86. Give a presentation about a product you are selling

87. Sell compact discs at a music store

88. Manage the operations of a hotel

89. Sell houses

90. Manage a supermarket

91. Sell a soft drink product line to stores and restaurants

92. Sell refreshments at a movie theater

93. Sell hair-care products to stores and salons

94. Start your own business

95. Negotiate business contracts

96. Represent a client in a lawsuit

97. Negotiate contracts for professional athletes

98. Market a new line of clothing

99. Sell automobiles

100. Sell computer equipment in a store

____ **Page Score for E**

(continued)

(continued)

Circle the numbers of the activities you would LIKE to do.

101. Develop a spreadsheet using computer software

102. Proofread records or forms

103. Use a computer program to generate customer bills

104. Schedule conferences for an organization

105. Keep accounts payable/receivable for an office

106. Load computer software into a large computer network

107. Organize and schedule office meetings

108. Use a word processor to edit and format documents

109. Direct or transfer phone calls for a large organization

110. Perform office filing tasks

111. Compute and record statistical and other numerical data

112. Take notes during a meeting

113. Calculate the wages of employees

114. Assist senior-level accountants in performing bookkeeping tasks

115. Inventory supplies using a handheld computer

116. Keep records of financial transactions for an organization

117. Record information from customers applying for charge accounts

118. Photocopy letters and reports

119. Stamp, sort, and distribute mail for an organization

120. Handle customers' bank transactions

____ **Page Score for C**

Step 2: Score Your Responses

Do the following to score your responses:

1. **Score the responses on each page.** On each page of responses, go from top to bottom and count how many numbers are circled. Then write that total in the "Page Score" box at the bottom of the page. Go on to the next page and do the same there.

2. **Determine your primary interest area.** Which Page Score has your highest score: **R, I, A, S, E,** or **C**? Enter the letter for that personality type on the following line.

   My Primary Personality Type: ___

   You will use your Primary Personality Type *first* to explore careers. (If two Page Scores are tied for the highest scores or are within 4 points of each other, use both of them for your Primary Personality Type. You are equally divided between two types.) Here are the definitions of the six types.

   R=Realistic. Realistic personalities like work activities that include practical, hands-on problems and solutions. They enjoy dealing with plants; animals; and real-world materials like wood, tools, and machinery. They enjoy outside work. Often they do not like occupations that mainly involve doing paperwork or working closely with others.

   I=Investigative. Investigative personalities like work activities that have to do with ideas and thinking more than with physical activity. They like to search for facts and figure out problems mentally rather than to persuade or lead people.

   A=Artistic. Artistic personalities like work activities that deal with the artistic side of things, such as forms, designs, and patterns. They like self-expression in their work. They prefer settings where work can be done without following a clear set of rules.

   S=Social. Social personalities like work activities that assist others and promote learning and personal development. They prefer to communicate more than to work with objects, machines, or data. They like to teach, to give advice, to help, or otherwise to be of service to people.

   E=Enterprising. Enterprising personalities like work activities having to do with starting up and carrying out projects, especially business ventures. They like persuading and leading people and making decisions. They like taking risks for profit. These personalities prefer action rather than thought.

C=**Conventional.** Conventional personalities like work activities that follow set procedures and routines. They prefer working with data and details rather than with ideas. They prefer work in which there are precise standards rather than work in which you have to judge things by yourself. These personalities like working where the lines of authority are clear.

3. **Determine your secondary interest areas.** Which Page Score has your next highest score? Which has your third highest score? Enter the letters for those areas in the following spaces.

My Secondary Personality Types: ___ ___

(If you do not find many occupations that you like using your Primary Personality Type, you can use your Secondary Personality Types to look at more career options.)

Step 3: Find Jobs That Suit Your Personality Type

Start with your Primary Personality Type and find matching jobs in the following table, which is organized according to the six personality types ("RIASEC"). When you find a job that interests you, turn to chapter 5, which is ordered by personality type and then by education and training, and read the job snapshot for that job. Another strategy is to turn directly to the section of chapter 5 that covers your Primary Personality Type and browse the descriptions of all the jobs in that section. Don't rule out a job just because the title is not familiar to you.

If you want to find jobs that *combine* your Primary Personality Type and a Secondary Personality Type, look in the following table for RIASEC codes that match the two codes. For example, if your Primary Personality Type is Investigative and your Secondary Personality Type is Realistic, you would look for jobs in the table coded IR—and you would find three, such as Nuclear Medicine Technologists. You will also find jobs coded IR_, such as Respiratory Therapists (coded IRS) and Computer Security Specialists (coded IRC). If you look further you'll find still more jobs coded I_R, such as Computer Support Specialists (coded ICR). All of these jobs are worth considering. Finally, to cast an even wider net, you may want to consider *reversing* the codes you're looking for. In the current example, you might look for jobs coded RI or RI_, such as Radiologic Technologists (coded RIS). But you need to keep in mind that these jobs may not be quite as satisfying because your Primary Personality Type, though represented, does not dominate.

Occupation Name	RIASEC Code(s)
Construction Carpenters	R
Helpers—Production Workers	R
Highway Maintenance Workers	R
Landscaping and Groundskeeping Workers	R
Painters, Construction and Maintenance	R
Septic Tank Servicers and Sewer Pipe Cleaners	R
Radiologic Technologists	RIS
Medical and Clinical Laboratory Technicians	RIC
Desktop Publishers	RA
Forest Fire Fighters	RS
Municipal Fire Fighters	RS
Bus Drivers, Transit and Intercity	RSC
Surgical Technologists	RSC
Forest Fire Fighting and Prevention Supervisors	RES
Municipal Fire Fighting and Prevention Supervisors	RES
Railroad Conductors and Yardmasters	REC
Construction Laborers	RC
Hazardous Materials Removal Workers	RC
Industrial Truck and Tractor Operators	RC
Laborers and Freight, Stock, and Material Movers, Hand	RC
Maintenance and Repair Workers, General	RC
Medical Equipment Preparers	RC
Rough Carpenters	RC
Tile and Marble Setters	RC
Truck Drivers, Heavy and Tractor-Trailer	RC
Truck Drivers, Light or Delivery Services	RC
Radiologic Technicians	RCI

(continued)

R=Realistic; I=Investigative; A=Artistic; S=Social; E=Enterprising; C=Conventional

(continued)

Occupation Name	RIASEC Code(s)
Medical and Clinical Laboratory Technologists	IR
Network Systems and Data Communications Analysts	IR
Nuclear Medicine Technologists	IR
Cardiovascular Technologists and Technicians	IRS
Respiratory Therapists	IRS
Computer Security Specialists	IRC
Computer Software Engineers, Applications	IRC
Computer Software Engineers, Systems Software	IRC
Physician Assistants	IS
Computer Support Specialists	ICR
Computer Systems Analysts	ICR
Database Administrators	ICR
Forensic Science Technicians	ICR
Compensation, Benefits, and Job Analysis Specialists	ICE
Costume Attendants	ARS
Technical Writers	AI
Athletic Trainers	SR
Dental Assistants	SR
Nursing Aides, Orderlies, and Attendants	SR
Occupational Therapist Assistants	SR
Occupational Therapists	SR
Physical Therapist Aides	SR
Physical Therapist Assistants	SR
Vocational Education Teachers, Postsecondary	SR
Emergency Medical Technicians and Paramedics	SRI
Radiation Therapists	SRI
Animal Trainers	SRE

R=Realistic; I=Investigative; A=Artistic; S=Social; E=Enterprising; C=Conventional

Occupation Name	RIASEC Code(s)
Fitness Trainers and Aerobics Instructors	SRE
Medical and Public Health Social Workers	SI
Registered Nurses	SI
Kindergarten Teachers, Except Special Education	SA
Preschool Teachers, Except Special Education	SA
Self-Enrichment Education Teachers	SA
Special Education Teachers, Preschool, Kindergarten, and Elementary School	SA
Elementary School Teachers, Except Special Education	SAI
Secondary School Teachers, Except Special and Vocational Education	SAI
Social and Community Service Managers	SE
Employment Interviewers	SEC
Personal Financial Advisors	SEC
Security Guards	SEC
Training and Development Specialists	SEC
Dental Hygienists	SC
Medical Assistants	SC
Residential Advisors	SC
Social and Human Service Assistants	SC
Teacher Assistants	SC
Athletes and Sports Competitors	ERS
Coaches and Scouts	ERS
First-Line Supervisors/Managers of Food Preparation and Serving Workers	ERC
Public Relations Specialists	EAS
Personnel Recruiters	ES
Sales Representatives, Wholesale and Manufacturing, Except Technical and Scientific Products	ES

(continued)

R=Realistic; I=Investigative; A=Artistic; S=Social; E=Enterprising; C=Conventional

(continued)

Occupation Name	RIASEC Code(s)
First-Line Supervisors/Managers of Retail Sales Workers	EC
Gaming Managers	EC
Paralegals and Legal Assistants	EC
Appraisers, Real Estate	ECS
First-Line Supervisors/Managers of Office and Administrative Support Workers	ECS
Meeting and Convention Planners	ECS
Medical Records and Health Information Technicians	C
Office Clerks, General	C
Pharmacy Technicians	CR
Shipping, Receiving, and Traffic Clerks	CR
Construction and Building Inspectors	CRI
Interviewers, Except Eligibility and Loan	CSE
Accountants	CE
Assessors	CE
Auditors	CE
Bill and Account Collectors	CE
Bookkeeping, Accounting, and Auditing Clerks	CE
Executive Secretaries and Administrative Assistants	CE
Tellers	CE
Customer Service Representatives	CES
Receptionists and Information Clerks	CES

R=Realistic; I=Investigative; A=Artistic; S=Social; E=Enterprising; C=Conventional

Key Points: Chapter 4

- A useful way to narrow down your options is by identifying the jobs that are a good fit for your personality.
- Your personality may be described by one, two, or even three types.

Chapter 5

Quick Snapshots of Today's Hot Jobs

Here you can get the basic facts about 100 hot jobs with the highest growth or openings through 2014. The jobs are ordered by the RIASEC personality types described in chapter 4, and within each type they are ordered by the level of education and training they require. They are ordered alphabetically within each level. So find the personality type that describes you best, choose a level of education or training that you might be comfortable aspiring toward, and look at the jobs included. You probably also want to look at the personality type that is of secondary relevance to you.

As you read each job snapshot, think about how much the job appeals to you. The personality type is only one factor to consider. Look at the specific work tasks. Do you think you can learn them and enjoy them? Are there any work conditions that you'd rather avoid? How does the pay compare to that of other jobs you're considering?

Even with all the facts presented here, you can get only a snapshot of the job. When you find one that is especially appealing, take the time to explore it in greater depth.

You wouldn't buy a car based on a snapshot. You'd be wise to talk to people who own the model, and you'd certainly take the car for a test drive. Likewise, to learn about a job you should talk to people working in that field and find out what they like and dislike about it, how they got started, and where they expect the best opportunities. "Test-drive" the job by visiting the worksite and seeing what it looks like, sounds like, and even smells like up close.

The appendix also has several suggestions for resources that will help you learn more about these hot jobs.

If you find a job here that particularly appeals to you and your further investigation proves it to be a good choice for you, start thinking about how to prepare for it. Chapter 6 has some useful pointers about how you can cut the time and expense of education and training.

It is helpful to identify and explore an additional job that interests you. Students seeking college admission often apply to one college that seems like a good fit and another that's a "safety school." You may be able to use a similar strategy and explore two jobs for the time being. Later, when you learn more about the jobs, you can decide which one is your best bet.

Realistic Jobs Requiring Short-Term On-the-Job Training

Helpers—Production Workers

- Level of Education/Training: Short-term on-the-job training
- Annual Earnings: $20,390
- Growth: 7.9%
- Annual Job Openings: 107,000
- Personality Type: Realistic (R)

These job opportunities are sensitive to ups and downs in the economy.

On the Job—Help production workers by performing duties of lesser skill. Duties include supplying or holding materials or tools and cleaning work areas and equipment. Observe equipment operations so that malfunctions can be detected and notify operators of any malfunctions. Operate machinery used in the production process or assist machine operators. Pack and store materials and products. Start machines or equipment to begin production processes. Break up defective products for reprocessing. Unclamp and hoist full reels from braiding, winding, and other fabricating machines, using power hoists. Signal co-workers to direct them to move products during the production process. Separate products according to weight, grade, size, and composition of materials used to produce them. Record information such as the number of products tested, meter readings, and dates and times of product production. Perform minor repairs to machines, such as replacing damaged or worn parts. Pack food products in paper bags and boxes and stack them in warehouses and coolers. Measure amounts of products, lengths of extruded articles, or weights of filled containers to ensure conformance to specifications. Fold products and product parts during processing. Examine products to verify conformance to quality standards. Read gauges and charts and record data obtained. Change machine gears, using wrenches. Thread ends of items such as thread, cloth, and lace through needles and rollers and around take-up tubes. Wash work areas, machines, equipment, vehicles, and products. Turn valves to regulate flow of liquids or air, to reverse machines, to start pumps, or to regulate equipment. Transfer finished products, raw materials, tools, or equipment between storage and work areas of plants and warehouses by hand or by using hand trucks or powered lift trucks. Tie products in bundles for further processing or shipment, following prescribed procedures. Remove products, machine attachments, and waste material from machines. Prepare raw materials for processing. Position spouts or chutes of storage bins so that containers can be filled. Place products in equipment or on work surfaces for further processing, inspecting, or wrapping. Mix ingredients according to specified procedures and formulas.

Hottest Fields Where They Work—Employment Services; Food Manufacturing.

Work Conditions—Indoors; hazardous equipment; standing; using hands on objects, tools, or controls; bending or twisting the body; repetitive motions.

Industrial Truck and Tractor Operators

- Level of Education/Training: Short-term on-the-job training
- Annual Earnings: $27,080
- Growth: 7.9%
- Annual Job Openings: 114,000
- Personality Type: Realistic (RC)

Workers must receive specialized training in safety awareness and procedures and be evaluated at least once every three years.

On the Job—Operate industrial trucks or tractors equipped to move materials around a warehouse, storage yard, factory, construction site, or similar location. Move controls to drive gasoline- or electric-powered trucks, cars, or tractors and transport materials between loading, processing, and storage areas. Move levers and controls that operate lifting devices, such as forklifts, lift beams and swivel-hooks, hoists, and elevating platforms, to load, unload, transport, and stack material. Position lifting devices under, over, or around loaded pallets, skids, and boxes and secure material or products for transport to designated areas. Manually load or unload materials onto or off pallets, skids, platforms, cars, or lifting devices. Perform routine maintenance on vehicles and auxiliary equipment, such as cleaning, lubricating, recharging batteries, fueling, or replacing liquefied-gas tank. Weigh materials or products and record weight and other production data on tags or labels. Operate or tend automatic stacking, loading, packaging, or cutting machines. Signal workers to discharge, dump, or level materials. Hook tow trucks to trailer hitches and fasten attachments such as graders, plows, rollers, and winch cables to tractors, using hitchpins. Turn valves and open chutes to dump, spray, or release materials from dump cars or storage bins into hoppers.

Hottest Fields Where They Work—Truck Transportation and Warehousing; Employment Services; Wholesale Trade.

Work Conditions—Noisy; very hot or cold; contaminants; standing; using hands on objects, tools, or controls; bending or twisting the body.

Laborers and Freight, Stock, and Material Movers, Hand

- Level of Education/Training: Short-term on-the-job training
- Annual Earnings: $20,610
- Growth: 10.2%
- Annual Job Openings: 671,000
- Personality Type: Realistic (RC)

Many openings will arise from the need to replace workers who transfer to other occupations or those who retire or leave the labor force for other reasons.

On the Job—Manually move freight, stock, or other materials or perform other unskilled general labor. Includes all unskilled manual laborers not elsewhere classified. Attach identifying tags to containers or mark them with identifying information. Read work orders or receive oral instructions to determine work assignments and material and equipment needs. Record numbers of units handled and moved, using daily production sheets or work tickets. Move freight, stock, and other materials to and from storage and production areas, loading docks, delivery vehicles, ships, and containers by hand or by using trucks, tractors, and other equipment. Sort cargo before loading and unloading. Assemble product containers and crates, using hand tools and precut lumber. Load and unload ship cargo, using winches and other hoisting devices. Connect hoses and operate equipment to move liquid materials into and out of storage tanks on vessels. Pack containers and re-pack damaged containers. Carry needed tools and supplies from storage or trucks and return them after use. Install protective devices, such as bracing, padding, or strapping, to prevent shifting or damage to items being transported. Maintain equipment storage areas to ensure that inventory is protected. Attach slings, hooks, and other devices to lift cargo and guide loads. Carry out general yard duties such as performing shunting on railway lines. Adjust controls to guide, position, and move equipment such as cranes, booms, and cameras. Guide loads being lifted to prevent swinging. Adjust or replace equipment parts such as rollers, belts, plugs, and caps, using hand tools. Stack cargo in locations such as transit sheds or in holds of ships as directed, using pallets or cargo boards. Connect electrical equipment to power sources so that it can be tested before use. Set up the equipment needed to produce special lighting and sound effects during performances. Bundle and band material such as fodder and tobacco leaves, using banding machines. Rig and dismantle props and equipment such as frames, scaffolding, platforms, or backdrops, using hand tools. Check out, rent, or requisition all equipment needed for productions or for set construction. Direct spouts and position receptacles such as bins, carts, and containers so they can be loaded.

Hottest Fields Where They Work—Employment Services; Truck Transportation and Warehousing.

Work Conditions—Outdoors; noisy; very hot or cold; contaminants; standing; using hands on objects, tools, or controls.

Landscaping and Groundskeeping Workers

- Level of Education/Training: Short-term on-the-job training
- Annual Earnings: $20,670
- Growth: 19.5%
- Annual Job Openings: 243,000
- Personality Type: Realistic (R)

Opportunities should be very good, especially for workers willing to work seasonal or variable schedules, because of significant job turnover and increasing demand by landscaping services companies.

On the Job—**Landscape or maintain grounds of property, using hand or power tools or equipment. Workers typically perform a variety of tasks, which may include any combination of the following: sod laying, mowing, trimming, planting, watering, fertilizing, digging, raking, sprinkler installation, and installation of mortarless segmental concrete masonry wall units.** Operate powered equipment such as mowers, tractors, twin-axle vehicles, snowblowers, chain saws, electric clippers, sod cutters, and pruning saws. Mow and edge lawns, using power mowers and edgers. Shovel snow from walks, driveways, and parking lots and spread salt in those areas. Care for established lawns by mulching; aerating; weeding; grubbing and removing thatch; and trimming and edging around flowerbeds, walks, and walls. Use hand tools such as shovels, rakes, pruning saws, saws, hedge and brush trimmers, and axes. Prune and trim trees, shrubs, and hedges, using shears, pruners, or chain saws. Maintain and repair tools; equipment; and structures such as buildings, greenhouses, fences, and benches, using hand and power tools. Gather and remove litter. Mix and spray or spread fertilizers, herbicides, or insecticides onto grass, shrubs, and trees, using hand or automatic sprayers or spreaders. Provide proper upkeep of sidewalks, driveways, parking lots, fountains, planters, burial sites, and other grounds features. Water lawns, trees, and plants, using portable sprinkler systems, hoses, or watering cans. Trim and pick flowers and clean flowerbeds. Rake, mulch, and compost leaves. Plant seeds, bulbs, foliage, flowering plants, grass, ground covers, trees, and shrubs and apply mulch for protection, using gardening tools. Follow planned landscaping designs to determine where to lay sod, sow grass, or plant flowers and foliage. Decorate gardens with stones and plants. Maintain irrigation systems, including winterizing the systems and starting them up in spring. Care for natural turf fields, making sure the underlying soil has the required composition to allow proper drainage and to support the grasses used on the fields. Use irrigation methods to adjust the amount of water consumption and to prevent waste. Haul or spread topsoil and spread straw over seeded soil to hold soil in place. Advise customers on plant selection and care. Care for artificial turf fields, periodically removing the turf and replacing cushioning pads and vacuuming and disinfecting the turf after use to prevent the growth of harmful bacteria.

Hottest Fields Where They Work—Arts, Entertainment, and Recreation; Employment Services; State and Local Government, Excluding Education and Hospitals; Educational Services; Hotels and Other Accommodations.

Work Conditions—Outdoors; noisy; very hot or cold; contaminants; standing; using hands on objects, tools, or controls.

Medical Equipment Preparers

- Level of Education/Training: Short-term on-the-job training
- Annual Earnings: $24,880
- Growth: 20.0%
- Annual Job Openings: 8,000
- Personality Type: Realistic (RC)

Employers typically offer training sessions to keep these technicians' skills up to date.

On the Job—**Prepare, sterilize, install, or clean laboratory or healthcare equipment. May perform routine laboratory tasks and operate or inspect equipment.** Organize and assemble routine and specialty surgical instrument trays and other sterilized supplies, filling special requests as needed. Clean instruments to prepare them for sterilization. Operate and maintain steam autoclaves, keeping records of loads completed, items in loads, and maintenance procedures performed. Record sterilizer test results. Disinfect and sterilize equipment such as respirators, hospital beds, and oxygen and dialysis equipment, using sterilizers, aerators, and washers. Start equipment and observe gauges and equipment operation to detect malfunctions and to ensure equipment is operating to prescribed standards. Examine equipment to detect leaks, worn or loose parts, or other indications of disrepair. Report defective equipment to appropriate supervisors or staff. Check sterile supplies to ensure that they are not outdated. Maintain records of inventory and equipment usage. Attend hospital in-service programs related to areas of work specialization. Purge wastes from equipment by connecting equipment to water sources and flushing water through systems. Deliver equipment to specified hospital locations or to patients' residences. Assist hospital staff with patient care duties such as providing transportation or setting up traction. Install and set up medical equipment, using hand tools.

Hottest Field Where They Work—Health Care

Work Conditions—Indoors; contaminants; disease or infections; standing; using hands on objects, tools, or controls; repetitive motions.

Truck Drivers, Light or Delivery Services

- Level of Education/Training: Short-term on-the-job training
- Annual Earnings: $24,790
- Growth: 15.7%
- Annual Job Openings: 169,000
- Personality Type: Realistic (RC)

Competition is expected for jobs offering the highest earnings or most favorable work schedules.

On the Job—Drive a truck or van with a capacity of under 26,000 GVW, primarily to deliver or pick up merchandise or to deliver packages within a specified area. May require use of automatic routing or location software. May load and unload truck. Obey traffic laws and follow established traffic and transportation procedures. Inspect and maintain vehicle supplies and equipment such as gas, oil, water, tires, lights, and brakes to ensure that vehicles are in proper working condition. Report any mechanical problems encountered with vehicles. Present bills and receipts and collect payments for goods delivered or loaded. Load and unload trucks, vans, or automobiles. Turn in receipts and money received from deliveries. Verify the contents of inventory loads against shipping papers. Maintain records such as vehicle logs, records of cargo, or billing statements in accordance with regulations. Read maps and follow written and verbal geographic directions. Report delays, accidents, or other traffic and transportation situations to bases or other vehicles, using telephones or mobile two-way radios. Sell and keep records of sales for products from truck inventory. Drive vehicles with capacities under three tons to transport materials to and from specified destinations such as railroad stations, plants, residences, and offices or within industrial yards. Drive trucks equipped with public address systems through city streets to broadcast announcements for advertising or publicity purposes. Use and maintain the tools and equipment found on commercial vehicles, such as weighing and measuring devices. Perform emergency repairs such as changing tires or installing light bulbs, fuses, tire chains, and spark plugs.

Hottest Fields Where They Work—Wholesale Trade; Employment Services; Truck Transportation and Warehousing; Food Services and Drinking Places; Construction.

Work Conditions—Outdoors; very hot or cold; contaminants; cramped work space, awkward positions; minor burns, cuts, bites, or stings; using hands on objects, tools, or controls.

Realistic Jobs Requiring Moderate-Term On-the-Job Training

Bus Drivers, Transit and Intercity

- Level of Education/Training: Moderate-term on-the-job training
- Annual Earnings: $31,010
- Growth: 21.7%
- Annual Job Openings: 34,000
- Personality Type: Realistic (RSC)

State and federal governments establish bus driver qualifications and standards, which include a commercial driver's license.

On the Job—Drive bus or motor coach, including regular route operations, charters, and private carriage. May assist passengers with baggage. May collect fares or tickets. Inspect vehicles and check gas, oil, and water levels prior to departure. Drive vehicles over specified routes or to specified destinations according to time schedules to transport passengers, complying with traffic regulations. Park vehicles at loading areas so that passengers can board. Assist passengers with baggage and collect tickets or cash fares. Report delays or accidents. Advise passengers to be seated and orderly while on vehicles. Regulate heating, lighting, and ventilating systems for passenger comfort. Load and unload baggage in baggage compartments. Record cash receipts and ticket fares. Make minor repairs to vehicle and change tires.

Hottest Field Where They Work—State and Local Government, Excluding Education and Hospitals.

Work Conditions—Outdoors; noisy; contaminants; sitting; using hands on objects, tools, or controls; repetitive motions.

Construction Laborers

- Level of Education/Training: Moderate-term on-the-job training
- Annual Earnings: $25,410
- Growth: 5.9%
- Annual Job Openings: 245,000
- Personality Type: Realistic (RC)

With training and experience, construction laborers can move into other skilled craft occupations.

On the Job—Perform tasks involving physical labor at building, highway, and heavy construction projects; tunnel and shaft excavations; and demolition sites. May operate hand and power tools of all types: air hammers, earth tampers, cement mixers, small mechanical hoists, surveying and measuring equipment, and a variety of other equipment and instruments. May clean and prepare sites; dig trenches; set braces to support the sides of excavations; erect scaffolding; clean up rubble and debris; and remove asbestos, lead, and other hazardous waste materials. May assist other craft workers. Install sewer, water, and storm drain pipes, using pipe-laying machinery and laser guidance equipment. Position, join, align, and seal structural components, such as concrete wall sections and pipes. Apply caulking compounds by hand or by using caulking guns. Build and position forms for pouring concrete and dismantle forms after use, using saws, hammers, nails, or bolts. Clean and prepare construction sites to eliminate possible hazards. Control traffic passing near, in, and around work zones. Dig ditches or trenches, backfill excavations, and compact and level earth to grade specifications, using picks, shovels, pneumatic tampers, and rakes. Erect and disassemble scaffolding, shoring, braces, traffic barricades, ramps, and other temporary structures. Grind, scrape, sand, or polish surfaces such as concrete, marble, terrazzo, or wood flooring, using abrasive tools or machines. Load, unload, and identify building materials, machinery, and tools and distribute them to the appropriate locations according to project plans and specifications. Measure, mark, and record openings and distances to lay out areas where construction work will be performed. Mix ingredients to create compounds for covering or cleaning surfaces. Mop, brush, or spread paints, cleaning solutions, or other compounds over surfaces to clean them or to provide protection. Place, consolidate, and protect case-in-place concrete or masonry structures. Lubricate, clean, and repair machinery, equipment, and tools. Shovel cement and other materials into portable cement mixers and mix, pour, and spread concrete. Signal equipment operators to facilitate alignment, movement, and adjustment of machinery, equipment, and materials. Smooth and finish freshly poured cement or concrete, using floats, trowels, screeds, or powered cement-finishing tools. Spray materials such as water, sand, steam, vinyl, paint, or stucco through hoses to clean, coat, or seal surfaces. Tend machines that pump concrete, grout, cement, sand, plaster, or stucco through spray guns for application to ceilings and walls. Tend pumps, compressors, and generators to provide power for tools, machinery, and equipment or to heat and move materials such as asphalt.

Hottest Fields Where They Work—Employment Services; Construction.

Work Conditions—Outdoors; noisy; contaminants; hazardous equipment; standing; using hands on objects, tools, or controls.

Hazardous Materials Removal Workers

- Level of Education/Training: Moderate-term on-the-job training
- Annual Earnings: $33,690
- Growth: 31.2%
- Annual Job Openings: 11,000
- Personality Type: Realistic (RC)

Formal education beyond high school is not required, but a training program leading to a federal license is mandatory.

On the Job—Identify, remove, pack, transport, or dispose of hazardous materials, including asbestos, lead-based paint, waste oil, fuel, transmission fluid, radioactive materials, contaminated soil, etc. Specialized training and certification in hazardous materials handling or a confined entry permit is generally required. May operate earth-moving equipment or trucks. Construct scaffolding or build containment areas prior to beginning abatement or decontamination work. Operate cranes to move and load baskets, casks, and canisters. Unload baskets of irradiated elements onto packaging machines that automatically insert fuel elements into canisters and secure lids. Remove asbestos or lead from surfaces, using hand and power tools such as scrapers, vacuums, and high-pressure sprayers. Pull tram cars along underwater tracks and position cars to receive irradiated fuel elements; then pull loaded cars to mechanisms that automatically unload elements onto underwater tables. Package, store, and move irradiated fuel elements in the underwater storage basin of a nuclear reactor plant, using machines and equipment. Manipulate handgrips of mechanical arms to place irradiated fuel elements into baskets. Apply chemical compounds to lead-based paint, allow compounds to dry, and then scrape the hazardous material into containers for removal or storage. Record numbers of containers stored at disposal sites and specify amounts and types of equipment and waste disposed. Operate machines and equipment to remove, package, store, or transport loads of waste materials. Mix and pour concrete into forms to encase waste material for disposal. Clean contaminated equipment or areas for reuse, using detergents and solvents, sandblasters, filter pumps, and steam cleaners. Follow prescribed safety procedures and comply with federal laws regulating waste disposal methods. Identify asbestos, lead, or other hazardous materials that need to be removed, using monitoring devices. Load and unload materials into containers and onto trucks, using hoists or forklifts. Drive trucks or other heavy equipment to convey contaminated waste to designated sea or ground locations. Organize and track the locations of hazardous items in landfills.

Hottest Fields Where They Work—State and Local Government, Excluding Education and Hospitals; Employment Services; Construction; Educational Services.

Work Conditions—Outdoors; contaminants; radiation; more often standing than sitting; using hands on objects, tools, or controls.

Highway Maintenance Workers

- Level of Education/Training: Moderate-term on-the-job training
- Annual Earnings: $30,250
- Growth: 23.3%
- Annual Job Openings: 27,000
- Personality Type: Realistic (R)

Some employers want applicants who have some experience in the construction or maintenance field. The experience requirement may be as short as six months or up to one year.

On the Job—Maintain highways, municipal and rural roads, airport runways, and rights of way. Duties include patching broken or eroded pavement and repairing guardrails, highway markers, and snow fences. May also mow or clear brush from along road or plow snow from roadway. Flag motorists to warn them of obstacles or repair work ahead. Set out signs and cones around work areas to divert traffic. Drive trucks or tractors with adjustable attachments to sweep debris from paved surfaces, mow grass and weeds, and remove snow and ice. Dump, spread, and tamp asphalt, using pneumatic tampers, to repair joints and patch broken pavement. Drive trucks to transport crews and equipment to worksites. Inspect, clean, and repair drainage systems, bridges, tunnels, and other structures. Haul and spread sand, gravel, and clay to fill washouts and repair road shoulders. Erect, install, or repair guardrails, road shoulders, berms, highway markers, warning signals, and highway lighting, using hand tools and power tools. Remove litter and debris from roadways, including debris from rock and mud slides. Clean and clear debris from culverts, catch basins, drop inlets, ditches, and other drain structures. Perform roadside landscaping work, such as clearing weeds and brush and planting and trimming trees. Paint traffic control lines and place pavement traffic messages by hand or by using machines. Inspect markers to verify accurate installation. Apply poisons along roadsides and in animal burrows to eliminate unwanted roadside vegetation and rodents. Measure and mark locations for installation of markers, using tape, string, or chalk. Apply oil to road surfaces, using sprayers. Blend compounds to form adhesive mixtures used for marker installation. Place and remove snow fences used to prevent the accumulation of drifting snow on highways.

Hottest Field Where They Work—State and Local Government, Excluding Education and Hospitals.

Work Conditions—Outdoors; noisy; very hot or cold; contaminants; hazardous equipment; using hands on objects, tools, or controls.

Maintenance and Repair Workers, General

- Level of Education/Training: Moderate-term on-the-job training
- Annual Earnings: $31,210
- Growth: 15.2%
- Annual Job Openings: 154,000
- Personality Type: Realistic (RC)

Many workers learn their skills informally on the job; others learn by working as helpers to other repairers or to construction workers such as carpenters, electricians, or machinery repairers.

On the Job—**Perform work involving the skills of two or more maintenance or craft occupations to keep machines, mechanical equipment, or the structure of an establishment in repair. Duties may involve pipe fitting; boiler making; insulating; welding; machining; carpentry; repairing electrical or mechanical equipment; installing, aligning, and balancing new equipment; and repairing buildings, floors, or stairs.** Repair or replace defective equipment parts, using hand tools and power tools, and reassemble equipment. Perform routine preventive maintenance to ensure that machines continue to run smoothly, building systems operate efficiently, and the physical condition of buildings does not deteriorate. Inspect drives, motors, and belts; check fluid levels; replace filters; and perform other maintenance actions, following checklists. Use tools ranging from common hand and power tools, such as hammers, hoists, saws, drills, and wrenches, to precision measuring instruments and electrical and electronic testing devices. Assemble, install, and repair wiring, electrical and electronic components, pipe systems and plumbing, machinery, and equipment. Diagnose mechanical problems and determine how to correct them, checking blueprints, repair manuals, and parts catalogs as necessary. Inspect, operate, and test machinery and equipment to diagnose machine malfunctions. Record maintenance and repair work performed and the costs of the work. Clean and lubricate shafts, bearings, gears, and other parts of machinery. Dismantle devices to gain access to and remove defective parts, using hoists, cranes, hand tools, and power tools. Plan and lay out repair work, using diagrams, drawings, blueprints, maintenance manuals, and schematic diagrams. Adjust functional parts of devices and control instruments, using hand tools, levels, plumb bobs, and straightedges. Order parts, supplies, and equipment from catalogs and suppliers or obtain them from storerooms. Paint and repair roofs, windows, doors, floors, woodwork, plaster, drywall, and other parts of building structures. Operate cutting torches or welding equipment to cut or join metal parts. Align and balance new equipment after installation. Inspect used parts to determine changes in dimensional requirements, using rules, calipers, micrometers, and other measuring instruments. Set up and operate machine tools to repair or fabricate machine parts, jigs and fixtures, and tools. Maintain and repair specialized equipment and machinery found in cafeterias, laundries, hospitals, stores, offices, and factories.

Hottest Fields Where They Work—Health Care; Educational Services; Hotels and Other Accommodations; State and Local Government, Excluding Education and Hospitals; Employment Services.

Work Conditions—Indoors; noisy; minor burns, cuts, bites, or stings; standing; walking and running; using hands on objects, tools, or controls.

Painters, Construction and Maintenance

- Level of Education/Training: Moderate-term on-the-job training
- Annual Earnings: $30,800
- Growth: 12.6%
- Annual Job Openings: 102,000
- Personality Type: Realistic (R)

Most workers learn informally on the job as helpers, but training experts recommend completion of an apprenticeship program.

On the Job—Paint walls, equipment, buildings, bridges, and other structural surfaces, using brushes, rollers, and spray guns. May remove old paint to prepare surface prior to painting. May mix colors or oils to obtain desired color or

consistency. Bake finishes on painted and enameled articles, using baking ovens. Cut stencils and brush and spray lettering and decorations on surfaces. Erect scaffolding and swing gates or set up ladders to work above ground level. Select and purchase tools and finishes for surfaces to be covered, considering durability, ease of handling, methods of application, and customers' wishes. Spray or brush hot plastics or pitch onto surfaces. Smooth surfaces, using sandpaper, scrapers, brushes, steel wool, or sanding machines. Waterproof buildings, using waterproofers and caulking. Remove old finishes by stripping, sanding, wire-brushing, burning, or using water or abrasive blasting. Use special finishing techniques such as sponging, ragging, layering, or faux finishing. Calculate amounts of required materials and estimate costs based on surface measurements or work orders. Wash and treat surfaces with oil, turpentine, mildew remover, or other preparations and sand rough spots to ensure that finishes will adhere properly. Apply primers or sealers to prepare new surfaces, such as bare wood or metal, for finish coats. Cover surfaces with dropcloths or masking tape and paper to protect surfaces during painting. Fill cracks, holes, and joints with caulk, putty, plaster, or other fillers, using caulking guns or putty knives. Mix and match colors of paint, stain, or varnish with oil and thinning and drying additives to obtain desired colors and consistencies. Polish final coats to specified finishes. Read work orders or receive instructions from supervisors or homeowners to determine work requirements. Remove fixtures such as pictures, doorknobs, lamps, and electric switch covers prior to painting. Apply paint, stain, varnish, enamel, and other finishes to equipment, buildings, bridges, or other structures, using brushes, spray guns, or rollers.

Hottest Fields Where They Work—Construction; Employment Services.

Work Conditions—Indoors; contaminants; high places; standing; using hands on objects, tools, or controls; repetitive motions.

Septic Tank Servicers and Sewer Pipe Cleaners

- Level of Education/Training: Moderate-term on-the-job training
- Annual Earnings: $30,440
- Growth: 21.8%
- Annual Job Openings: 3,000
- Personality Type: Realistic (R)

Many openings are created by the replacement of current workers because the working conditions are often considered unpleasant.

On the Job—Clean and repair septic tanks, sewer lines, or drains. May patch walls and partitions of tank, replace damaged drain tile, or repair breaks in underground piping. Communicate with supervisors and other workers, using equipment such as wireless phones, pagers, or radio telephones. Inspect manholes to locate sewer line stoppages. Break asphalt and other pavement so that pipes can be accessed, using airhammers, picks, and shovels. Cut damaged sections of pipe with cutters; remove broken sections from ditches; and replace pipe sections, using pipe sleeves. Dig out sewer lines manually, using shovels. Drive trucks to transport crews, materials, and equipment. Prepare and keep records of actions taken, including maintenance and repair work. Requisition or order tools and equipment. Service, adjust, and make minor repairs to equipment, machines, and attachments. Locate problems, using specially designed equipment, and mark where digging must occur to reach damaged tanks or pipes. Withdraw cables from pipes and examine them for evidence of mud, roots, grease, and other deposits indicating broken or clogged sewer lines. Update sewer maps and manhole charts. Cover repaired pipes with dirt and pack backfilled excavations, using air and gasoline tampers. Install rotary knives on flexible cables mounted on machine reels according to the diameters of pipes to be cleaned. Tap mainline sewers to install sewer saddles. Start machines to feed revolving cables or rods into openings, stopping machines and changing knives to conform to pipe sizes. Rotate cleaning rods manually, using turning pins. Operate sewer cleaning equipment, including power rodders, high-velocity water jets, sewer flushers, bucket machines, wayne balls, and vac-alls. Measure excavation sites, using plumbers' snakes, tapelines, or lengths of cutting heads within sewers, and mark areas for digging. Ensure that repaired sewer line joints are tightly sealed before backfilling begins. Clean and repair septic tanks; sewer lines; or related structures such as manholes, culverts, and catch basins. Clean and disinfect domestic basements and other areas flooded by sewer stoppages.

Hottest Fields Where They Work—State and Local Government, Excluding Education and Hospitals; Construction; Utilities.

Work Conditions—Outdoors; contaminants; standing; kneeling, crouching, stooping, or crawling; using hands on objects, tools, or controls; bending or twisting the body.

Truck Drivers, Heavy and Tractor-Trailer

- Level of Education/Training: Moderate-term on-the-job training
- Annual Earnings: $34,280
- Growth: 12.9%
- Annual Job Openings: 274,000
- Personality Type: Realistic (RC)

A commercial driver's license is required to operate most larger trucks.

On the Job—Drive a tractor-trailer combination or a truck with a capacity of at least 26,000 GVW to transport and deliver goods, livestock, or materials in liquid, loose, or packaged form. May be required to unload truck. May require use of automated routing equipment. Requires commercial drivers' license. Follow appropriate safety procedures when transporting dangerous goods. Check vehicles before driving them to ensure that mechanical, safety, and emergency equipment is in good working order. Maintain logs of working hours and of vehicle service and repair status, following applicable state and federal regulations. Obtain receipts or signatures when loads are delivered and collect payment for services when required. Check all load-related documentation to ensure that it is complete and accurate. Maneuver trucks into loading or unloading positions, following signals from loading crew as needed; check that vehicle position is correct and any special loading equipment is properly positioned. Drive trucks with capacities greater than 3 tons, including tractor-trailer combinations, to transport and deliver products, livestock, or other materials. Secure cargo for transport, using ropes, blocks, chain, binders, or covers. Read bills of lading to determine assignment details. Report vehicle defects, accidents, traffic violations, or damage to the vehicles. Read and interpret maps to determine vehicle routes. Couple and uncouple trailers by changing trailer jack positions, connecting or disconnecting air and electrical lines, and manipulating fifth-wheel locks. Collect delivery instructions from appropriate sources, verifying instructions and routes. Drive trucks to weigh stations before and after loading and along routes to document weights and to comply with state regulations. Operate equipment such as truck cab computers, CB radios, and telephones to exchange necessary information with bases, supervisors, or other drivers. Check conditions of trailers after contents have been unloaded to ensure that there has been no damage. Crank trailer landing gear up and down to safely secure vehicles. Wrap goods, using pads, packing paper, and containers, and secure loads to trailer walls, using straps. Perform basic vehicle maintenance tasks such as adding oil, fuel, and radiator fluid or performing minor repairs. Load and unload trucks or help others with loading and unloading, operating any special loading-related equipment on vehicles and using other equipment as necessary.

Hottest Fields Where They Work—Truck Transportation and Warehousing; Employment Services; Wholesale Trade; Construction.

Work Conditions—Outdoors; very hot or cold; contaminants; sitting; using hands on objects, tools, or controls; repetitive motions.

Realistic Jobs Requiring Long-Term On-the-Job Training

Construction Carpenters

- Level of Education/Training: Long-term on-the-job training
- Annual Earnings: $35,580
- Growth: 13.8%
- Annual Job Openings: 210,000
- Personality Type: Realistic (R)

The job openings listed here are shared with Rough Carpenters.

> About one-third of all carpenters—the largest construction trade—were self-employed.

On the Job—**Construct, erect, install, and repair structures and fixtures of wood, plywood, and wallboard, using carpenter's hand tools and power tools.** Measure and mark cutting lines on materials, using ruler, pencil, chalk, and marking gauge. Follow established safety rules and regulations and maintain a safe and clean environment. Verify trueness of structure, using plumb bob and level. Shape or cut materials to specified measurements, using hand tools, machines, or power saw. Study specifications in blueprints, sketches, or building plans to prepare project layout and determine dimensions and materials required. Assemble and fasten materials to make framework or props, using hand tools and wood screws, nails, dowel pins, or glue. Build or repair cabinets, doors, frameworks, floors, and other wooden fixtures used in buildings, using woodworking machines, carpenter's hand tools, and power tools. Erect scaffolding and ladders for assembling structures above ground level. Remove damaged or defective parts or sections of structures and repair or replace, using hand tools. Install structures and fixtures, such as windows, frames, floorings, and trim, or hardware, using carpenter's hand and power tools. Select and order lumber and other required materials. Maintain records, document actions, and present written progress reports. Finish surfaces of woodwork or wallboard in houses and buildings, using paint, hand tools, and paneling. Prepare cost estimates for clients or employers. Arrange for subcontractors to deal with special areas such as heating and electrical wiring work. Inspect ceiling or floor tile, wall coverings, siding, glass, or woodwork to detect broken or damaged structures. Work with or remove hazardous material. Construct forms and chutes for pouring concrete. Cover subfloors with building paper to keep out moisture and lay hardwood, parquet, and wood-strip-block floors by nailing floors to subfloor or cementing them to mastic or asphalt base. Fill cracks and other defects in plaster or plasterboard and sand patch, using patching plaster, trowel, and sanding tool. Perform minor plumbing, welding, or concrete mixing work. Apply shock-absorbing, sound-deadening, and decorative paneling to ceilings and walls.

Hottest Fields Where They Work—Construction; Employment Services.

Work Conditions—Outdoors; noisy; hazardous equipment; standing; walking and running; using hands on objects, tools, or controls.

Forest Fire Fighters

- Level of Education/Training: Long-term on-the-job training
- Annual Earnings: $39,090
- Growth: 24.3%
- Annual Job Openings: 21,000
- Personality Type: Realistic (RS)

The job openings listed here are shared with Municipal Fire Fighters.

Fighting forest fires is rigorous work and involves hazardous conditions and long, irregular hours.

On the Job—Control and suppress fires in forests or vacant public land. Maintain contact with fire dispatchers at all times to notify them of the need for additional firefighters and supplies or to detail any difficulties encountered. Rescue fire victims and administer emergency medical aid. Collaborate with other fire-fighters as a member of a firefighting crew. Patrol burned areas after fires to locate and eliminate hot spots that may restart fires. Extinguish flames and embers to suppress fires, using shovels or engine- or hand-driven water or chemical pumps. Fell trees, cut and clear brush, and dig trenches to create firelines, using axes, chain saws, or shovels. Maintain knowledge of current firefighting practices by participating in drills and by attending seminars, conventions, and conferences. Operate pumps connected to high-pressure hoses. Participate in physical training to maintain high levels of physical fitness. Establish water supplies, connect hoses, and direct water onto fires. Maintain fire equipment and firehouse living quarters. Inform and educate the public about fire prevention. Take action to contain any hazardous chemicals that could catch fire, leak, or spill. Organize fire caches, positioning equipment for the most effective response. Transport personnel and cargo to and from fire areas. Participate in fire prevention and inspection programs. Perform forest maintenance and improvement tasks such as cutting brush, planting trees, building trails, and marking timber. Test and maintain tools, equipment, jump gear, and parachutes to ensure readiness for fire suppression activities. Observe forest areas from fire lookout towers to spot potential problems. Orient self in relation to fire, using compass and map, and collect supplies and equipment dropped by parachute. Serve as fully trained lead helicopter crewmember and as helispot manager. Drop weighted paper streamers from aircraft to determine the speed and direction of the wind at fire sites.

Hottest Field Where They Work—State and Local Government, Excluding Education and Hospitals.

Work Conditions—Outdoors; very hot or cold; contaminants; hazardous conditions; minor burns, cuts, bites, or stings; using hands on objects, tools, or controls.

Municipal Fire Fighters

- Level of Education/Training: Long-term on-the-job training
- Annual Earnings: $39,090
- Growth: 24.3%
- Annual Job Openings: 21,000
- Personality Type: Realistic (RS)

The job openings listed here are shared with Forest Fire Fighters.

Applicants for municipal fire fighting jobs generally must pass written, physical, and medical examinations.

On the Job—Control and extinguish municipal fires, protect life and property, and conduct rescue efforts. Administer first aid and cardiopulmonary resuscitation to injured persons. Rescue victims from burning buildings and accident sites. Search burning buildings to locate fire victims. Drive and operate fire fighting vehicles and equipment. Move toward the source of a fire, using knowledge of types of fires, construction design, building materials, and physical layout of properties. Dress with equipment such as fire-resistant clothing and breathing apparatus. Position and climb ladders to gain access to upper levels of buildings or to rescue individuals from burning structures. Take action to contain hazardous chemicals that might catch fire, leak, or spill. Assess fires and situations and report conditions to superiors to receive instructions, using two-way radios. Respond to fire alarms and other calls for assistance, such as automobile and industrial accidents. Operate pumps connected to high-pressure hoses. Select and attach hose nozzles, depending on fire type, and direct streams of water or chemicals onto fires. Create openings in buildings for ventilation or entrance, using axes, chisels, crowbars, electric saws, or core cutters. Inspect fire sites after flames have been extinguished to ensure that there is no further danger. Lay hose lines and connect them to water supplies. Protect property from water and smoke, using waterproof salvage covers, smoke ejectors, and deodorants. Participate in physical training activities to maintain a high level of physical fitness. Salvage property by removing broken glass, pumping out water, and ventilating buildings to remove smoke. Participate in fire drills and demonstrations of fire fighting techniques. Clean and maintain fire stations and fire fighting equipment and apparatus. Collaborate with police to respond to accidents, disasters, and arson investigation calls. Establish firelines to prevent unauthorized persons from entering areas near fires. Inform and educate the public on fire prevention. Inspect buildings for fire hazards and compliance with fire prevention ordinances, testing and checking smoke alarms and fire suppression equipment as necessary.

Hottest Field Where They Work—State and Local Government, Excluding Education and Hospitals.

Work Conditions—More often outdoors than indoors; noisy; contaminants; disease or infections; hazardous equipment.

Rough Carpenters

- Level of Education/Training: Long-term on-the-job training
- Annual Earnings: $35,580
- Growth: 13.8%
- Annual Job Openings: 210,000
- Personality Type: Realistic (RC)

The job openings listed here are shared with Construction Carpenters.

Job opportunities should be excellent for those with the most training and all-around skills.

On the Job—**Build rough wooden structures, such as concrete forms; scaffolds; tunnel, bridge, or sewer supports; billboard signs; and temporary frame shelters, according to sketches, blueprints, or oral instructions.** Study blueprints and diagrams to determine dimensions of structure or form to be constructed. Measure materials or distances, using square, measuring tape, or rule to lay out work. Cut or saw boards, timbers, or plywood to required size, using handsaw, power saw, or woodworking machine. Assemble and fasten material together to construct wood or metal framework of structure, using bolts, nails, or screws. Anchor and brace forms and other structures in place, using nails, bolts, anchor rods, steel cables, planks, wedges, and timbers. Mark cutting lines on materials, using pencil and scriber. Erect forms, framework, scaffolds, hoists, roof supports, or chutes, using hand tools, plumb rule, and level. Install rough door and window frames, sub-flooring, fixtures, or temporary supports in structures undergoing construction or repair. Examine structural timbers and supports to detect decay and replace timbers as required, using hand tools, nuts, and bolts. Bore boltholes in timber, masonry, or concrete walls, using power drill. Fabricate parts, using woodworking and metalworking machines. Dig or direct digging of post holes and set poles to support structures. Build sleds from logs and timbers for use in hauling camp buildings and machinery through wooded areas. Build chutes for pouring concrete.

Hottest Fields Where They Work—Construction; Employment Services.

Work Conditions—Outdoors; noisy; very hot or cold; contaminants; standing; using hands on objects, tools, or controls.

Tile and Marble Setters

- Level of Education/Training: Long-term on-the-job training
- Annual Earnings: $36,530
- Growth: 22.9%
- Annual Job Openings: 9,000
- Personality Type: Realistic (RC)

Apprenticeship programs and some contractor-sponsored programs provide comprehensive training in all phases of the trade.

On the Job—**Apply hard tile, marble, and wood tile to walls, floors, ceilings, and roof decks.** Align and straighten tile, using levels, squares and straightedges. Determine and implement the best layout to achieve a desired pattern. Cut and shape tile to fit around obstacles and into odd spaces and corners, using hand and power cutting tools. Finish and dress the joints and wipe excess grout from between tiles, using damp sponge. Apply mortar to tile back, position the tile, and press or tap with trowel handle to affix tile to base. Mix, apply, and spread plaster, concrete, mortar, cement, mastic, glue, or other adhesives to form a bed for the tiles, using brush, trowel, and screed. Prepare cost and labor estimates based on calculations of time and materials needed for project. Measure and mark surfaces to be tiled, following blueprints. Level concrete and allow to dry. Build underbeds and install anchor bolts, wires, and brackets. Prepare surfaces for tiling by attaching lath or waterproof paper or by applying a cement mortar coat onto a metal screen. Study blueprints and examine surface to be covered to determine amount of material needed. Cut, surface, polish, and install marble and granite or install pre-cast terrazzo, granite, or marble units. Install and anchor fixtures in designated positions, using hand tools. Cut tile backing to required size, using shears. Remove any old tile, grout, and adhesive, using chisels and scrapers, and clean the surface carefully. Lay and set mosaic tiles to create decorative wall, mural, and floor designs. Assist customers in selection of tile and grout. Remove and replace cracked or damaged tile. Measure and cut metal lath to size for walls and ceilings, using tin snips. Select and order tile and other items to be installed, such as bathroom accessories, walls, panels, and cabinets, according to specifications. Mix and apply mortar or cement to edges and ends of drain tiles to seal halves and joints. Spread mastic or other adhesive base on roof deck to form base for promenade tile, using serrated spreader. Apply a sealer to make grout stain- and water-resistant. Brush glue onto manila paper on which design has been drawn and position tiles, finished side down, onto paper.

Hottest Field Where They Work—Construction.

Work Conditions—Noisy; contaminants; cramped work space, awkward positions; standing; using hands on objects, tools, or controls; bending or twisting the body.

Realistic Jobs Requiring Work Experience in a Related Occupation

Forest Fire Fighting and Prevention Supervisors

- Level of Education/Training: Work experience in a related occupation
- Annual Earnings: $60,840
- Growth: 21.1%
- Annual Job Openings: 4,000
- Personality Type: Realistic (RES)

The job openings listed here are shared with Municipal Fire Fighting and Prevention Supervisors.

Opportunities for promotion depend upon the results of written examinations, as well as job performance, interviews, and seniority.

On the Job—Supervise fire fighters who control and suppress fires in forests or vacant public land. Communicate fire details to superiors, subordinates, and interagency dispatch centers, using two-way radios. Serve as working leader of an engine-, hand-, helicopter-, or prescribed fire crew of three or more firefighters. Maintain fire suppression equipment in good condition, checking equipment periodically to ensure that it is ready for use. Evaluate size, location, and condition of forest fires in order to request and dispatch crews and position equipment so fires can be contained safely and effectively. Operate wildland fire engines and hoselays. Direct and supervise prescribed burn projects and prepare post-burn reports analyzing burn conditions and results. Monitor prescribed burns to ensure that they are conducted safely and effectively. Identify staff training and development needs to ensure that appropriate training can be arranged. Maintain knowledge of forest fire laws and fire prevention techniques and tactics. Recommend equipment modifications or new equipment purchases. Perform administrative duties such as compiling and maintaining records, completing forms, preparing reports, and composing correspondence. Recruit and hire forest fire–fighting personnel. Train workers in such skills as parachute jumping, fire suppression, aerial observation, and radio communication both in the classroom and on the job. Review and evaluate employee performance. Observe fires and crews from air to determine fire-fighting force requirements and to note changing conditions that will affect fire-fighting efforts. Inspect all stations, uniforms, equipment, and recreation areas to ensure compliance with safety standards, taking corrective action as necessary. Schedule employee work assignments and set work priorities. Regulate open burning by issuing burning permits, inspecting problem sites, issuing citations for violations of laws and ordinances, and educating the public in proper burning practices. Direct investigations of suspected arsons in wildfires, working closely with other investigating agencies. Monitor fire suppression expenditures to ensure that they are necessary and reasonable.

Hottest Fields Where They Work—State and Local Government, Excluding Education and Hospitals; Federal Government, Excluding the Postal Service.

Work Conditions—Outdoors; noisy; very hot or cold; hazardous equipment; minor burns, cuts, bites, or stings; standing.

Municipal Fire Fighting and Prevention Supervisors

- Level of Education/Training: Work experience in a related occupation
- Annual Earnings: $60,840
- Growth: 21.1%
- Annual Job Openings: 4,000
- Personality Type: Realistic (RES)

The job openings listed here are shared with Forest Fire Fighting and Prevention Supervisors.

To progress to supervisory positions, fire fighters acquire expertise in advanced fire fighting equipment and techniques, building construction, emergency medical technology, writing, public speaking, management and budgeting procedures, and public relations.

On the Job—Supervise fire fighters who control and extinguish municipal fires, protect life and property, and conduct rescue efforts. Assign firefighters to jobs at strategic locations to facilitate rescue of persons and maximize application of extinguishing agents. Provide emergency medical services as required and perform light to heavy rescue functions at emergencies. Assess nature and extent of fire, condition of building, danger to adjacent buildings, and water supply status to determine crew or company requirements. Instruct and drill fire department personnel in assigned duties, including firefighting, medical care, hazardous materials response, fire prevention, and related subjects. Evaluate the performance of assigned firefighting personnel. Direct the training of firefighters, assigning of instructors to training classes, and providing of supervisors with reports on training progress and status. Prepare activity reports listing fire call locations, actions taken, fire types and probable causes, damage estimates, and situation dispositions. Maintain required maps and records. Attend in-service training classes to remain current in knowledge of codes, laws, ordinances, and regulations. Evaluate fire station procedures to ensure efficiency and enforcement of departmental regulations. Direct firefighters in station maintenance duties and participate in these duties. Compile and maintain equipment and personnel records, including accident reports. Direct investigation of cases of suspected arson, hazards, and false alarms and submit reports outlining findings. Recommend personnel actions related to disciplinary procedures, performance, leaves of absence, and grievances. Supervise and participate in the inspection of properties to ensure that they are in compliance with applicable fire codes, ordinances, laws, regulations, and standards. Write and submit proposals for repair, modification, or replacement of firefighting equipment. Coordinate the distribution of fire prevention promotional materials. Identify corrective actions needed to bring properties into compliance with applicable fire codes and ordinances and conduct follow-up inspections to see if corrective actions have been taken. Participate in creating fire safety guidelines and evacuation schemes for non-residential buildings.

Hottest Fields Where They Work—State and Local Government, Excluding Education and Hospitals; Federal Government, Excluding the Postal Service.

Work Conditions—More often outdoors than indoors; noisy; contaminants; disease or infections; hazardous equipment.

Railroad Conductors and Yardmasters

- Level of Education/Training: Work experience in a related occupation
- Annual Earnings: $54,040
- Growth: 20.3%
- Annual Job Openings: 3,000
- Personality Type: Realistic (REC)

Most workers begin as yard laborers and later may have the opportunity to train for engineer or conductor jobs.

On the Job—Conductors coordinate activities of train crew on passenger or freight train. Coordinate activities of switch-engine crew within yard of railroad, industrial plant, or similar location. Yardmasters coordinate activities of workers engaged in railroad traffic operations, such as the makeup or breakup of trains, yard switching, and review of train schedules and switching orders. Signal engineers to begin train runs, stop trains, or change speed, using telecommunications equipment or hand signals. Receive information regarding train or rail problems from dispatchers or from electronic monitoring devices. Direct and instruct workers engaged in yard activities, such as switching tracks, coupling and uncoupling cars, and routing inbound and outbound traffic. Keep records of the contents and destination of each train car and make sure that cars are added or removed at proper points on routes. Operate controls to activate track switches and traffic signals. Instruct workers to set warning signals in front and at rear of trains during emergency stops. Direct engineers to move cars to fit planned train configurations, combining or separating cars to make up or break up trains. Receive instructions from dispatchers regarding trains' routes, timetables, and cargoes. Review schedules, switching orders, way bills, and shipping records to obtain cargo loading and unloading information and to plan work. Confer with engineers regarding train routes, timetables, and cargoes and to discuss alternative routes when there are rail defects or obstructions. Arrange for the removal of defective cars from trains at stations or stops. Inspect each car periodically during runs. Observe yard traffic to determine tracks available to accommodate inbound and outbound traffic. Document and prepare reports of accidents, unscheduled stops, or delays. Confirm routes and destination information for freight cars. Supervise and coordinate crew activities to transport freight and passengers and to provide boarding, porter, maid, and meal services to passengers. Supervise workers in the inspection and maintenance of mechanical equipment to ensure efficient and safe train operation. Record departure and arrival times, messages, tickets and revenue collected, and passenger accommodations and destinations. Inspect freight cars for compliance with sealing procedures and record car numbers and seal numbers. Collect tickets, fares, or passes from passengers. Verify accuracy of timekeeping instruments with engineers to ensure trains depart on time.

Hottest Field Where They Work—State and Local Government, Excluding Education and Hospitals.

Work Conditions—Outdoors; noisy; very hot or cold; very bright or dim lighting; contaminants; hazardous equipment.

Realistic Jobs Requiring Postsecondary Vocational Training

Desktop Publishers

- Level of Education/Training: Postsecondary vocational training
- Annual Earnings: $32,800
- Growth: 23.2%
- Annual Job Openings: 8,000
- Personality Type: Realistic (RA)

Most employers prefer to hire experienced desktop publishers; among persons without experience, opportunities should be best for those with certificates or degrees in desktop publishing or graphic design.

On the Job—Format typescript and graphic elements, using computer software, to produce publication-ready material. Check preliminary and final proofs for errors and make necessary corrections. Operate desktop publishing software and equipment to design, lay out, and produce camera-ready copy. View monitors for visual representation of work in progress and for instructions and feedback throughout process, making modifications as necessary. Enter text into computer keyboard and select the size and style of type, column width, and appropriate spacing for printed materials. Store copies of publications on paper, magnetic tape, film, or diskette. Position text and art elements from a variety of databases in a visually appealing way to design print or Web pages, using knowledge of type styles and size and layout patterns. Enter digitized data into electronic prepress system computer memory, using scanner, camera, keyboard, or mouse. Edit graphics and photos, using pixel or bitmap editing, airbrushing, masking, or image retouching. Import text and art elements such as electronic clip art or electronic files from photographs that have been scanned or produced with a digital camera, using computer software. Prepare sample layouts for approval, using computer software. Study layout or other design instructions to determine work to be done and sequence of operations. Load floppy disks or tapes containing information into system. Convert various types of files for printing or for the Internet, using computer software. Enter data, such as coordinates of images and color specifications, into system to retouch and make color corrections. Select number of colors and determine color separations. Transmit, deliver, or mail publication master to printer for production into film and plates. Collaborate with graphic artists, editors, and writers to produce master copies according to design specifications. Create special effects such as vignettes, mosaics, and image combining and add elements such as sound and animation to electronic publications.

Hottest Fields Where They Work—Publishing, Except Software; Advertising and Public Relations Services; Management, Scientific, and Technical Consulting Services; Employment Services; Educational Services.

Work Conditions—Indoors; sitting; repetitive motions.

Educational Program—Prepress/Desktop Publishing and Digital Imaging Design.

Surgical Technologists

- Level of Education/Training: Postsecondary vocational training
- Annual Earnings: $34,830
- Growth: 29.5%
- Annual Job Openings: 12,000
- Personality Type: Realistic (RSC)

Training programs last 9 to 24 months and lead to a certificate, diploma, or associate degree.

On the Job—Assist in operations under the supervision of surgeons, registered nurses, or other surgical personnel. May help set up operating room; prepare and transport patients for surgery; adjust lights and equipment; pass instruments and other supplies to surgeons and surgeon's assistants; hold retractors; cut sutures; and help count sponges, needles, supplies, and instruments. Count sponges, needles, and instruments before and after operation. Hand instruments and supplies to surgeons and surgeons' assistants, hold retractors and cut sutures, and perform other tasks as directed by surgeon during operation. Scrub arms and hands and assist the surgical team to scrub and put on gloves, masks, and surgical clothing. Position patients on the operating table and cover them with sterile surgical drapes to prevent exposure. Provide technical assistance to surgeons, surgical nurses, and anesthesiologists. Wash and sterilize equipment, using germicides and sterilizers. Prepare, care for, and dispose of tissue specimens taken for laboratory analysis. Clean and restock the operating room, placing equipment and supplies and arranging instruments according to instruction. Prepare dressings or bandages and apply or assist with their application following surgery. Operate, assemble, adjust, or monitor sterilizers, lights, suction machines, and diagnostic equipment to ensure proper operation. Monitor and continually assess operating room conditions, including patient and surgical team needs. Observe patients' vital signs to assess physical condition. Maintain supply of fluids, such as plasma, saline, blood, and glucose, for use during operations. Maintain files and records of surgical procedures.

Hottest Field Where They Work—Health Care.

Work Conditions—Indoors; contaminants; disease or infections; hazardous conditions; standing; using hands on objects, tools, or controls.

Educational Programs—Pathology/Pathologist Assistant; Surgical Technology/ Technologist.

Realistic Jobs Requiring an Associate Degree

Medical and Clinical Laboratory Technicians

- Level of Education/Training: Associate degree
- Annual Earnings: $31,700
- Growth: 25.0%
- Annual Job Openings: 14,000
- Personality Type: Realistic (RIC)

These technicians generally have either an associate degree from a community or junior college or a certificate from a hospital, a vocational or technical school, or one of the armed forces. A few technicians learn their skills on the job.

On the Job—Perform routine medical laboratory tests for the diagnosis, treatment, and prevention of disease. May work under the supervision of a medical technologist. Conduct chemical analyses of body fluids, such as blood and urine, using microscope or automatic analyzer to detect abnormalities or diseases, and enter findings into computer. Set up, adjust, maintain, and clean medical laboratory equipment. Analyze the results of tests and experiments to ensure conformity to specifications, using special mechanical and electrical devices. Analyze and record test data to issue reports that use charts, graphs, and narratives. Conduct blood tests for transfusion purposes and perform blood counts. Perform medical research to further control and cure disease. Obtain specimens, cultivating, isolating, and identifying microorganisms for analysis. Examine cells stained with dye to locate abnormalities. Collect blood or tissue samples from patients, observing principles of asepsis to obtain blood sample. Consult with a pathologist to determine a final diagnosis when abnormal cells are found. Inoculate fertilized eggs, broths, or other bacteriological media with organisms. Cut, stain, and mount tissue samples for examination by pathologists. Supervise and instruct other technicians and laboratory assistants. Prepare standard volumetric solutions and reagents to be combined with samples, following standardized formulas or experimental procedures. Prepare vaccines and serums by standard laboratory methods, testing for virus inactivity and sterility. Test raw materials, processes, and finished products to determine quality and quantity of materials or characteristics of a substance.

Hottest Fields Where They Work—Health Care; Educational Services.

Work Conditions—Indoors; disease or infections; standing; walking and running; using hands on objects, tools, or controls.

Educational Programs—Clinical/Medical Laboratory Assistant; Blood Bank Technology Specialist; Hematology Technology/Technician; Clinical/Medical Laboratory Technician; Histologic Technician.

Radiologic Technicians

- Level of Education/Training: Associate degree
- Annual Earnings: $45,950
- Growth: 23.2%
- Annual Job Openings: 17,000
- Personality Type: Realistic (RCI)

The job openings listed here are shared with Radiologic Technologists.

Although hospitals will remain the primary employer, a greater number of new jobs will be found in physicians' offices and diagnostic imaging centers.

On the Job—Maintain and use equipment and supplies necessary to demonstrate portions of the human body on X-ray film or fluoroscopic screen for diagnostic purposes. Use beam-restrictive devices and patient-shielding techniques to minimize radiation exposure to patient and staff. Position X-ray equipment and adjust controls to set exposure factors, such as time and distance. Position patient on examining table and set up and adjust equipment to obtain optimum view of specific body area as requested by physician. Determine patients' X-ray needs by reading requests or instructions from physicians. Make exposures necessary for the requested procedures, rejecting and repeating work that does not meet established standards. Process exposed radiographs, using film processors or computer-generated methods. Explain procedures to patients to reduce anxieties and obtain cooperation. Perform procedures such as linear tomography; mammography; sonograms;

joint and cyst aspirations; routine contrast studies; routine fluoroscopy; and examinations of the head, trunk, and extremities under supervision of physician. Prepare and set up X-ray room for patient. Assure that sterile supplies, contrast materials, catheters, and other required equipment are present and in working order, requisitioning materials as necessary. Maintain records of patients examined, examinations performed, views taken, and technical factors used. Provide assistance to physicians or other technologists in the performance of more complex procedures. Monitor equipment operation and report malfunctioning equipment to supervisor. Provide students and other technologists with suggestions of additional views, alternate positioning, or improved techniques to ensure the images produced are of the highest quality. Coordinate work of other technicians or technologists when procedures require more than one person. Assist with on-the-job training of new employees and students and provide input to supervisors regarding training performance. Maintain a current file of examination protocols. Operate mobile X-ray equipment in operating room, in emergency room, or at patient's bedside. Provide assistance in radiopharmaceutical administration, monitoring patients' vital signs and notifying the radiologist of any relevant changes.

Hottest Field Where They Work—Health Care.

Work Conditions—Indoors; radiation; disease or infections; standing; walking and running; using hands on objects, tools, or controls.

Educational Programs—Medical Radiologic Technology/Science—Radiation Therapist; Radiologic Technology/Science—Radiographer; Allied Health Diagnostic, Intervention, and Treatment Professions, Other.

Radiologic Technologists

- Level of Education/Training: Associate degree
- Annual Earnings: $45,950
- Growth: 23.2%
- Annual Job Openings: 17,000
- Personality Type: Realistic (RIS)

The job openings listed here are shared with Radiologic Technicians.

Job opportunities are expected to be favorable; some employers report difficulty hiring sufficient numbers of radiologic technologists.

On the Job—Take X rays and Computerized Axial Tomography (CAT or CT) scans or administer nonradioactive materials into patient's bloodstream for

diagnostic purposes. Includes technologists who specialize in other modalities, such as computed tomography, ultrasound, and magnetic resonance. Review and evaluate developed X rays, videotape, or computer-generated information to determine if images are satisfactory for diagnostic purposes. Use radiation safety measures and protection devices to comply with government regulations and to ensure safety of patients and staff. Explain procedures and observe patients to ensure safety and comfort during scan. Operate or oversee operation of radiologic and magnetic imaging equipment to produce images of the body for diagnostic purposes. Position and immobilize patient on examining table. Position imaging equipment and adjust controls to set exposure time and distance according to specification of examination. Key commands and data into computer to document and specify scan sequences, adjust transmitters and receivers, or photograph certain images. Monitor video display of area being scanned and adjust density or contrast to improve picture quality. Monitor patients' conditions and reactions, reporting abnormal signs to physician. Prepare and administer oral or injected contrast media to patients. Set up examination rooms, ensuring that all necessary equipment is ready. Take thorough and accurate patient medical histories. Remove and process film. Record, process, and maintain patient data and treatment records and prepare reports. Coordinate work with clerical personnel or other technologists. Demonstrate new equipment, procedures, and techniques to staff and provide technical assistance. Provide assistance in dressing or changing seriously ill, injured, or disabled patients. Move ultrasound scanner over patient's body and watch pattern produced on video screen. Measure thickness of section to be radiographed, using instruments similar to measuring tapes. Operate fluoroscope to aid physician to view and guide wire or catheter through blood vessels to area of interest. Assign duties to radiologic staff to maintain patient flows and achieve production goals. Collaborate with other medical team members, such as physicians and nurses, to conduct angiography or special vascular procedures. Perform administrative duties such as developing departmental operating budget, coordinating purchases of supplies and equipment, and preparing work schedules.

Hottest Field Where They Work—Health Care.

Work Conditions—Indoors; disease or infections; standing; walking and running; using hands on objects, tools, or controls; repetitive motions.

Educational Programs—Medical Radiologic Technology/Science—Radiation Therapist; Radiologic Technology/Science—Radiographer; Allied Health Diagnostic, Intervention, and Treatment Professions, Other.

Investigative Jobs Requiring an Associate Degree

Cardiovascular Technologists and Technicians

- Level of Education/Training: Associate degree
- Annual Earnings: $40,420
- Growth: 32.6%
- Annual Job Openings: 5,000
- Personality Type: Investigative (IRS)

Employment of most specialties will grow, but fewer EKG technicians will be needed.

On the Job—Conduct tests on pulmonary or cardiovascular systems of patients for diagnostic purposes. May conduct or assist in electrocardiograms, cardiac catheterizations, pulmonary-functions, lung capacity, and similar tests. Monitor patients' blood pressure and heart rate, using electrocardiogram (EKG) equipment during diagnostic and therapeutic procedures to notify the physician if something appears wrong. Monitor patients' comfort and safety during tests, alerting physicians to abnormalities or changes in patient responses. Explain testing procedures to patients to obtain cooperation and reduce anxiety. Prepare reports of diagnostic procedures for interpretation by physician. Observe gauges, recorder, and video screens of data analysis system during imaging of cardiovascular system. Conduct electrocardiogram (EKG), phonocardiogram, echocardiogram, stress testing, or other cardiovascular tests to record patients' cardiac activity, using specialized electronic test equipment, recording devices, and laboratory instruments. Obtain and record patient identification, medical history, or test results. Prepare and position patients for testing. Attach electrodes to patients' chests, arms, and legs; connect electrodes to leads from the electrocardiogram (EKG) machine; and operate the EKG machine to obtain a reading. Adjust equipment and controls according to physicians' orders or established protocol. Check, test, and maintain cardiology equipment, making minor repairs when necessary, to ensure proper operation. Supervise and train other cardiology technologists and students. Assist physicians in diagnosis and treatment of cardiac and peripheral vascular treatments; for example, assisting with balloon angioplasties to treat blood vessel blockages. Operate diagnostic imaging equipment to produce contrast-enhanced radiographs of heart and cardiovascular system. Inject contrast medium into patients' blood vessels. Observe ultrasound display screen and listen to signals to record vascular information such as blood pressure, limb volume changes, oxygen saturation, and cerebral circulation. Assess cardiac physiology and calculate valve areas from blood flow velocity measurements. Compare measurements of heart wall thickness and chamber sizes to standard norms to identify abnormalities. Activate fluoroscope and camera to produce images used to guide catheter through cardiovascular system.

Hottest Field Where They Work—Health Care.

Work Conditions—Indoors; radiation; disease or infections; standing; walking and running; using hands on objects, tools, or controls.

Educational Programs—Cardiovascular Technology/Technologist; Electrocardiograph Technology/Technician; Perfusion Technology/Perfusionist; Cardiopulmonary Technology/Technologist.

Computer Support Specialists

- Level of Education/Training: Associate degree
- Annual Earnings: $40,610
- Growth: 23.0%
- Annual Job Openings: 87,000
- Personality Type: Investigative (ICR)

Job prospects should be best for college graduates who are up to date with the latest skills and technologies; certifications and practical experience are essential for persons without degrees.

On the Job—Provide technical assistance to computer system users. Answer questions or resolve computer problems for clients in person, via telephone, or from remote location. May provide assistance concerning the use of computer hardware and software, including printing, installation, word processing, electronic mail, and operating systems. Answer user inquiries regarding computer software or hardware operation to resolve problems. Enter commands and observe system functioning to verify correct operations and detect errors. Install and perform minor repairs to hardware, software, or peripheral equipment, following design or installation specifications. Oversee the daily performance of computer systems. Set up equipment for employee use, performing or ensuring proper installation of cables, operating systems, or appropriate software. Maintain records of daily data communication transactions, problems and remedial actions taken, or installation activities. Read technical manuals, confer with users, or conduct computer diagnostics to investigate and resolve problems or to provide technical assistance and support. Confer with staff, users, and management to establish requirements for new systems or modifications. Develop training materials and procedures or train users in the proper use of hardware or software. Refer major hardware or software problems or defective products to vendors or technicians for service. Prepare evaluations of software or hardware and recommend improvements or upgrades. Read trade magazines and technical manuals or attend conferences and seminars to maintain knowledge of hardware and software. Supervise and coordinate workers engaged in problem-solving, monitoring, and installing data communication equipment and software. Inspect equipment and read order sheets to prepare for delivery to users. Modify and customize commercial programs for internal needs. Conduct office automation feasibility studies, including workflow analysis, space design, or cost comparison analysis.

Hottest Fields Where They Work—Computer Systems Design and Related Services; Educational Services; Software Publishers; Employment Services; Internet Service Providers, Web Search Portals, and Data Processing Services.

Work Conditions—Indoors; noisy; sitting; repetitive motions.

Educational Programs—Agricultural Business Technology; Data Processing and Data Processing Technology/Technician; Computer Hardware Technology/Technician; Computer Software Technology/Technician; Accounting and Computer Science; Medical Office Computer Specialist/Assistant.

Forensic Science Technicians

- Level of Education/Training: Associate degree
- Annual Earnings: $44,590
- Growth: 36.4%
- Annual Job Openings: 2,000
- Personality Type: Investigative (ICR)

Job seekers with a 4-year degree in a forensic science will enjoy much better opportunities than those with only a 2-year degree. Knowledge and understanding of legal procedures also can be helpful.

On the Job—Collect, identify, classify, and analyze physical evidence related to criminal investigations. Perform tests on weapons or substances such as fiber, hair, and tissue to determine significance to investigation. May testify as expert witnesses on evidence or crime laboratory techniques. May serve as specialists in area of expertise, such as ballistics, fingerprinting, handwriting, or biochemistry.** Testify in court about investigative and analytical methods and findings. Keep records and prepare reports detailing findings, investigative methods, and laboratory techniques. Interpret laboratory findings and test results to identify and classify substances, materials, and other evidence collected at crime scenes. Operate and maintain laboratory equipment and apparatus. Prepare solutions, reagents, and sample formulations needed for laboratory work. Analyze and classify biological fluids, using DNA typing or serological techniques. Collect evidence from crime scenes, storing it in conditions that preserve its integrity. Identify and quantify drugs and poisons found in biological fluids and tissues, in foods, and at crime scenes. Analyze handwritten and machine-produced textual evidence to decipher altered or obliterated text or to determine authorship, age, or source. Reconstruct crime scenes to determine relationships among pieces of evidence. Examine DNA samples to determine if they match other samples. Collect impressions of dust from surfaces to obtain and identify fingerprints. Analyze gunshot residue and bullet paths to determine how shootings occurred. Visit morgues, examine scenes of crimes, or contact other sources to obtain evidence or information to be used in investigations. Examine physical evidence such as hair, fiber, wood, or soil residues to obtain information about its source and composition. Determine types of bullets used in shooting and whether they were fired from a specific weapon. Examine firearms to determine mechanical condition and legal status, performing restoration work on damaged firearms to obtain information such as serial numbers. Confer with ballistics, fingerprinting, handwriting, documents, electronics, medical, chemical, or metallurgical experts concerning evidence and its interpretation. Interpret the pharmacological effects of a drug or a combination of drugs on an individual. Compare objects such as tools with impression marks to determine whether a specific object is responsible for a specific mark.

Hottest Field Where They Work—State and Local Government, Excluding Education and Hospitals.

Work Conditions—Indoors; contaminants; disease or infections; hazardous conditions; sitting.

Educational Program—Forensic Science and Technology.

Nuclear Medicine Technologists

- Level of Education/Training: Associate degree
- Annual Earnings: $59,670
- Growth: 21.5%
- Annual Job Openings: 2,000
- Personality Type: Investigative (IR)

Technologists who also are trained in other diagnostic methods, such as radiologic technology or diagnostic medical sonography, will have the best prospects.

On the Job—Prepare, administer, and measure radioactive isotopes in therapeutic, diagnostic, and tracer studies, utilizing a variety of radioisotope equipment. Prepare stock solutions of radioactive materials and calculate doses to be administered by radiologists. **Subject patients to radiation. Execute blood volume, red cell survival, and fat absorption studies, following standard laboratory techniques.** Calculate, measure, and record radiation dosage or radiopharmaceuticals received, used, and disposed, using computer and following physician's prescription. Detect and map radiopharmaceuticals in patients' bodies, using a camera to produce photographic or computer images. Explain test procedures and safety precautions to patients and provide them with assistance during test procedures. Administer radiopharmaceuticals or radiation to patients to detect or treat diseases, using radioisotope equipment, under direction of physician. Produce a computer-generated or film image for interpretation by a physician. Process cardiac function studies, using computer. Dispose of radioactive materials and store radiopharmaceuticals, following radiation safety procedures. Record and process results of procedures. Prepare stock radiopharmaceuticals, adhering to safety standards that minimize radiation exposure to workers and patients. Maintain and calibrate radioisotope and laboratory equipment. Gather information on patients' illnesses and medical history to guide the choice of diagnostic procedures for therapy. Measure glandular activity, blood volume, red cell survival, and radioactivity of patient, using scanners, Geiger counters, scintillometers, and other laboratory equipment. Train and supervise student or subordinate nuclear medicine technologists. Position radiation fields, radiation beams, and patient to allow for most effective treatment of patient's disease, using computer. Add radioactive substances to biological specimens, such as blood, urine, and feces, to determine therapeutic drug or hormone levels. Develop treatment procedures for nuclear medicine treatment programs.

Hottest Fields Where They Work—Health Care; Employment Services.

Work Conditions—Indoors; contaminants; radiation; disease or infections; standing; using hands on objects, tools, or controls.

Educational Programs—Nuclear Medical Technology/Technologist; Radiation Protection/Health Physics Technician.

Respiratory Therapists

- Level of Education/Training: Associate degree
- Annual Earnings: $45,140
- Growth: 28.4%
- Annual Job Openings: 7,000
- Personality Type: Investigative (IRS)

All states (except Alaska and Hawaii), the District of Columbia, and Puerto Rico require respiratory therapists to obtain a license.

On the Job—Assess, treat, and care for patients with breathing disorders. Assume primary responsibility for all respiratory care modalities, including the supervision of respiratory therapy technicians. Initiate and conduct therapeutic procedures; maintain patient records; and select, assemble, check, and operate equipment. Set up and operate devices such as mechanical ventilators, therapeutic gas administration apparatus, environmental control systems, and aerosol generators, following specified parameters of treatment. Provide emergency care, including artificial respiration, external cardiac massage, and assistance with cardio pulmonary resuscitation. Determine requirements for treatment, such as type, method, and duration of therapy; precautions to be taken; and medication and dosages, compatible with physicians' orders. Monitor patient's physiological responses to therapy, such as vital signs, arterial blood gases, and blood chemistry changes, and consult with physician if adverse reactions occur. Read prescription, measure arterial blood gases, and review patient information to assess patient condition. Work as part of a team of physicians, nurses, and other health care professionals to manage patient care. Enforce safety rules and ensure careful adherence to physicians' orders. Maintain charts that contain patients' pertinent identification and therapy information. Inspect, clean, test, and maintain respiratory therapy equipment to ensure equipment is functioning safely and efficiently, ordering repairs when necessary. Educate patients and their families about their conditions and teach appropriate disease management techniques, such as breathing exercises and the use of medications and respiratory equipment. Explain treatment procedures to patients to gain cooperation and allay fears. Relay blood analysis results to a physician. Perform pulmonary function and adjust equipment to obtain optimum results in therapy. Perform bronchopulmonary drainage and assist or instruct patients in performance of breathing exercises. Demonstrate respiratory care procedures to trainees and other health care personnel. Teach, train, supervise, and utilize the assistance of students, respiratory therapy technicians, and assistants. Make emergency visits to resolve equipment problems. Use a variety of testing techniques to assist doctors in cardiac and pulmonary research and to diagnose disorders. Conduct tests such as electrocardiograms (EKGs), stress testing, and lung capacity tests to evaluate patients' cardiopulmonary functions.

Hottest Field Where They Work—Health Care.

Work Conditions—Indoors; disease or infections; standing.

Educational Program—Respiratory Care Therapy/Therapist.

Investigative Jobs Requiring a Bachelor's Degree

Compensation, Benefits, and Job Analysis Specialists

- Level of Education/Training: Bachelor's degree
- Annual Earnings: $48,870
- Growth: 20.4%
- Annual Job Openings: 15,000
- Personality Type: Investigative (ICE)

> For many specialized jobs, previous experience is an asset. Many employers prefer entry-level workers who have gained some experience through an internship or work-study program while in school.

On the Job—Conduct programs of compensation and benefits and job analysis for employer. May specialize in specific areas, such as position classification and pension programs. Evaluate job positions, determining classification, exempt or non-exempt status, and salary. Ensure company compliance with federal and state laws, including reporting requirements. Advise managers and employees on state and federal employment regulations, collective agreements, benefit and compensation policies, personnel procedures, and classification programs. Plan, develop, evaluate, improve, and communicate methods and techniques for selecting, promoting, compensating, evaluating, and training workers. Provide advice on the resolution of classification and salary complaints. Prepare occupational classifications, job descriptions, and salary scales. Assist in preparing and maintaining personnel records and handbooks. Prepare reports such as organization and flow charts and career path reports to summarize job analysis and evaluation and compensation analysis information. Administer employee insurance, pension, and savings plans, working with insurance brokers and plan carriers. Negotiate collective agreements on behalf of employers or workers and mediate labor disputes and grievances. Develop, implement, administer, and evaluate personnel and labor relations programs, including performance appraisal, affirmative action, and employment equity programs. Perform multifactor data and cost analyses that may be used in areas such as support of collective bargaining agreements. Research employee benefit and health and safety practices and recommend changes or modifications to existing policies. Analyze organizational, occupational, and industrial data to facilitate organizational functions and provide technical information to business, industry, and government. Advise staff of individuals' qualifications. Assess need for and develop job analysis instruments and materials. Review occupational data on Alien Employment Certification Applications to determine the appropriate occupational title and code and provide local offices with information about immigration and occupations. Research job and worker requirements, structural and functional relationships among jobs and occupations, and occupational trends.

Hottest Fields Where They Work—State and Local Government, Excluding Education and Hospitals; Management, Scientific, and Technical Consulting Services; Insurance; Employment Services; Health Care.

Work Conditions—Indoors; noisy; sitting; using hands on objects, tools, or controls; repetitive motions.

Educational Programs—Human Resources Management/Personnel Administration, General; Labor and Industrial Relations.

Computer Security Specialists

- Level of Education/Training: Bachelor's degree
- Annual Earnings: $59,930
- Growth: 38.4%
- Annual Job Openings: 34,000
- Personality Type: Investigative (IRC)

The job openings listed here are shared with Network and Computer Systems Administrators.

Job prospects should be best for college graduates who are up to date with the latest skills and technologies; certifications and practical experience are essential for persons without degrees.

On the Job—Plan, coordinate, and implement security measures for information systems to regulate access to computer data files and prevent unauthorized modification, destruction, or disclosure of information. Train users and promote security awareness to ensure system security and to improve server and network efficiency. Develop plans to safeguard computer files against accidental or unauthorized modification, destruction, or disclosure and to meet emergency data processing needs. Confer with users to discuss issues such as computer data access needs, security violations, and programming changes. Monitor current reports of computer viruses to determine when to update virus protection systems. Modify computer security files to incorporate new software, correct errors, or change individual access status. Coordinate implementation of computer system plan with establishment personnel and outside vendors. Monitor use of data files and regulate access to safeguard information in computer files. Perform risk assessments and execute tests of data processing system to ensure functioning of data processing activities and security measures. Encrypt data transmissions and erect firewalls to conceal confidential information as it is being transmitted and to keep out tainted digital transfers. Document computer security and emergency measures policies, procedures, and tests. Review violations of computer security procedures and discuss procedures with violators to ensure violations are not repeated. Maintain permanent fleet cryptologic and carry-on direct support systems required in special land, sea surface, and subsurface operations.

Hottest Fields Where They Work—Computer Systems Design and Related Services; Educational Services; Internet Service Providers, Web Search Portals, and Data Processing Services; Wholesale Trade; State and Local Government, Excluding Education and Hospitals.

Work Conditions—Indoors; sitting.

Educational Programs—Computer and Information Sciences, General; Information Science/Studies; Computer Systems Analysis/Analyst; Computer Systems Networking and Telecommunications; System Administration/Administrator; System, Networking, and LAN/WAN Management/Manager; Computer and Information Systems Security; Computer and Information Sciences and Support Services, Other.

Computer Software Engineers, Applications

- Level of Education/Training: Bachelor's degree
- Annual Earnings: $77,090
- Growth: 48.4%
- Annual Job Openings: 54,000
- Personality Type: Investigative (IRC)

Very good opportunities are expected for college graduates with at least a bachelor's degree in computer engineering or computer science and with practical work experience.

On the Job—Develop, create, and modify general computer applications software or specialized utility programs. Analyze user needs and develop software solutions. Design software or customize software for client use with the aim of optimizing operational efficiency. May analyze and design databases within an application area, working individually or coordinating database development as part of a team. Confer with systems analysts, engineers, programmers, and others to design system and to obtain information on project limitations and capabilities, performance requirements, and interfaces. Modify existing software to correct errors, allow it to adapt to new hardware, or improve its performance. Analyze user needs and software requirements to determine feasibility of design within time and cost constraints. Consult with customers about software system design and maintenance. Coordinate software system installation and monitor equipment functioning to ensure specifications are met. Design, develop, and modify software systems, using scientific analysis and mathematical models to predict and measure outcome and consequences of design. Develop and direct software system testing and validation procedures, programming, and documentation. Analyze information to determine, recommend, and plan computer specifications and layouts and peripheral equipment modifications. Supervise the work of programmers, technologists and technicians, and other engineering and scientific personnel. Obtain and evaluate information on factors such as reporting formats required, costs, and security needs to determine hardware configuration. Determine system performance standards. Train users to use new or modified equipment. Store, retrieve, and manipulate data for analysis of system capabilities and requirements. Specify power supply requirements and configuration. Recommend purchase of equipment to control dust, temperature, and humidity in area of system installation.

Hottest Fields Where They Work—Computer Systems Design and Related Services; Software Publishers; Management, Scientific, and Technical Consulting Services; Internet Service Providers, Web Search Portals, and Data Processing Services.

Work Conditions—Indoors; sitting; using hands on objects, tools, or controls; repetitive motions.

Educational Programs—Artificial Intelligence and Robotics; Information Technology; Computer Science; Computer Engineering, General; Computer Software Engineering; Computer Engineering Technologies/Technicians, Other; Bioinformatics; Medical Informatics; Medical Illustration and Informatics, Other.

Computer Software Engineers, Systems Software

- Level of Education/Training: Bachelor's degree
- Annual Earnings: $82,120
- Growth: 43.0%
- Annual Job Openings: 37,000
- Personality Type: Investigative (IRC)

Computer software engineers must continually strive to acquire new skills in conjunction with the rapid changes that are occurring in computer technology.

On the Job—Research, design, develop, and test operating systems–level software, compilers, and network distribution software for medical, industrial, military, communications, aerospace, business, scientific, and general computing applications. Set operational specifications and formulate and analyze software requirements. Apply principles and techniques of computer science, engineering, and mathematical analysis. Modify existing software to correct errors, to adapt it to new hardware, or to upgrade interfaces and improve performance. Design and develop software systems, using scientific analysis and mathematical models to predict and measure outcome and consequences of design. Consult with engineering staff to evaluate interface between hardware and software, develop specifications and performance requirements, and resolve customer problems. Analyze information to determine, recommend, and plan installation of a new system or modification of an existing system. Develop and direct software system testing and validation procedures. Direct software programming and development of documentation. Consult with customers or other departments on project status, proposals, and technical issues such as software system design and maintenance. Advise customer about, or perform, maintenance of software system. Coordinate installation of software system. Monitor functioning of equipment to ensure system operates in conformance with specifications. Store, retrieve, and manipulate data for analysis of system capabilities and requirements. Confer with data processing and project managers to obtain information on limitations and capabilities for data processing projects. Prepare reports and correspondence concerning project specifications, activities, and status. Evaluate factors such as reporting formats required, cost constraints, and need for security restrictions to determine hardware configuration. Supervise and assign work to programmers, designers, technologists and technicians, and other engineering and scientific personnel. Train users to use new or modified equipment. Utilize microcontrollers to develop control signals; implement control algorithms;and measure process variables such as temperatures, pressures, and positions. Recommend purchase of equipment to control dust, temperature, and humidity in area of system installation. Specify power supply requirements and configuration.

Hottest Fields Where They Work—Computer Systems Design and Related Services; Software Publishers; Internet Service Providers, Web Search Portals, and Data Processing Services; Management, Scientific, and Technical Consulting Services; Wholesale Trade.

Work Conditions—Indoors; sitting; using hands on objects, tools, or controls; repetitive motions.

Educational Programs—Artificial Intelligence and Robotics; Information Technology; Information Science/Studies; Computer Science; System, Networking, and LAN/WAN Management/Manager; Computer Engineering, General; Computer Engineering Technologies/Technicians, Other.

Computer Systems Analysts

- Level of Education/Training: Bachelor's degree
- Annual Earnings: $68,300
- Growth: 31.4%
- Annual Job Openings: 56,000
- Personality Type: Investigative (ICR)

While there is no universally accepted way to prepare for this job, most employers place a premium on some formal college education.

On the Job—Analyze science, engineering, business, and all other data processing problems for application to electronic data processing systems. Analyze user requirements, procedures, and problems to automate or improve existing systems and review computer system capabilities, workflow, and scheduling limitations. May analyze or recommend commercially available software. May supervise computer programmers. Provide staff and users with assistance solving computer-related problems, such as malfunctions and program problems. Test, maintain, and monitor computer programs and systems, including coordinating the installation of computer programs and systems. Use object-oriented programming languages, client and server applications development processes, and multimedia and Internet technology. Confer with clients regarding the nature of the information processing or computation needs a computer program is to address. Coordinate and link the computer systems within an organization to increase compatibility and so information can be shared. Consult with management to ensure agreement on system principles. Expand or modify system to serve new purposes or improve work flow. Interview or survey workers, observe job performance, or perform the job to determine what information is processed and how it is processed. Determine computer software or hardware needed to set up or alter system. Train staff and users to work with computer systems and programs. Analyze information processing or computation needs and plan and design computer systems, using techniques such as structured analysis, data modeling, and information engineering. Assess the usefulness of pre-developed application packages and adapt them to a user environment. Define the goals of the system and devise flow charts and diagrams describing logical operational steps of programs. Develop, document, and revise system design procedures, test procedures, and quality standards. Review and analyze computer printouts and performance indicators to locate code problems and correct errors by correcting codes. Recommend new equipment or software packages. Read manuals, periodicals, and technical reports to learn how to develop programs that meet staff and user requirements. Supervise computer programmers or other systems analysts or serve as project leaders for particular systems projects. Utilize the computer in the analysis and solution of business problems such as development of integrated production and inventory control and cost analysis systems.

Hottest Fields Where They Work—Computer Systems Design and Related Services; Management, Scientific, and Technical Consulting Services; Educational Services; Internet Service Providers, Web Search Portals, and Data Processing Services; Insurance.

Work Conditions—Indoors; sitting.

Educational Programs—Computer and Information Sciences, General; Information Technology; Computer Systems Analysis/Analyst; Web/Multimedia Management and Webmaster.

Database Administrators

- Level of Education/Training: Bachelor's degree
- Annual Earnings: $63,250
- Growth: 38.2%
- Annual Job Openings: 9,000
- Personality Type: Investigative (ICR)

A bachelor's degree is a prerequisite for many jobs; however, some jobs may require only a 2-year degree. Relevant work experience also is very important.

On the Job—Coordinate changes to computer databases. Test and implement the database, applying knowledge of database management systems. May plan, coordinate, and implement security measures to safeguard computer databases. Develop standards and guidelines to guide the use and acquisition of software and to protect vulnerable information. Modify existing databases and database management systems or direct programmers and analysts to make changes. Test programs or databases, correct errors, and make necessary modifications. Plan, coordinate, and implement security measures to safeguard information in computer files against accidental or unauthorized damage, modification, or disclosure. Approve, schedule, plan, and supervise the installation and testing of new products and improvements to computer systems such as the installation of new databases. Train users and answer questions. Establish and calculate optimum values for database parameters, using manuals and calculator. Specify users and user access levels for each segment of database. Develop data model describing data elements and how they are used, following procedures and using pen, template, or computer software. Develop methods for integrating different products so they work properly together, such as customizing commercial databases to fit specific needs. Review project requests describing database user needs to estimate time and cost required to accomplish project. Review procedures in database management system manuals for making changes to database. Work as part of a project team to coordinate database development and determine project scope and limitations. Select and enter codes to monitor database performance and to create production database. Identify and evaluate industry trends in database systems to serve as a source of information and advice for upper management. Write and code logical and physical database descriptions and specify identifiers of database to management system or direct others in coding descriptions. Review workflow charts developed by programmer analyst to understand tasks computer will perform, such as updating records. Revise company definition of data as defined in data dictionary.

Hottest Fields Where They Work—Computer Systems Design and Related Services; Educational Services; Management, Scientific, and Technical Consulting Services; Internet Service Providers, Web Search Portals, and Data Processing Services; State and Local Government, Excluding Education and Hospitals.

Work Conditions—Indoors; noisy; sitting; using hands on objects, tools, or controls; repetitive motions.

Educational Programs—Computer and Information Sciences, General; Computer Systems Analysis/Analyst; Data Modeling/Warehousing and Database Administration; Computer and Information Systems Security; Management Information Systems, General.

Medical and Clinical Laboratory Technologists

- Level of Education/Training: Bachelor's degree
- Annual Earnings: $47,710
- Growth: 20.5%
- Annual Job Openings: 14,000
- Personality Type: Investigative (IR)

Job opportunities are expected to be excellent, as the volume of laboratory tests continues to increase with both population growth and the development of new types of tests.

On the Job—Perform complex medical laboratory tests for diagnosis, treatment, and prevention of disease. May train or supervise staff. Analyze laboratory findings to check the accuracy of the results. Conduct chemical analysis of body fluids, including blood, urine, and spinal fluid, to determine presence of normal and abnormal components. Operate, calibrate, and maintain equipment used in quantitative and qualitative analysis, such as spectrophotometers, calorimeters, flame photometers, and computer-controlled analyzers. Enter data from analysis of medical tests and clinical results into computer for storage. Analyze samples of biological material for chemical content or reaction. Establish and monitor programs to ensure the accuracy of laboratory results. Set up, clean, and maintain laboratory equipment. Provide technical information about test results to physicians, family members, and researchers. Supervise, train, and direct lab assistants, medical and clinical laboratory technicians and technologists, and other medical laboratory workers engaged in laboratory testing. Develop, standardize, evaluate, and modify procedures, techniques, and tests used in the analysis of specimens and in medical laboratory experiments. Cultivate, isolate, and assist in identifying microbial organisms and perform various tests on these microorganisms. Study blood samples to determine the number of cells and their morphology, as well as the blood group, type, and compatibility for transfusion purposes, using microscopic technique. Obtain, cut, stain, and mount biological material on slides for microscopic study and diagnosis, following standard laboratory procedures. Select and prepare specimen and media for cell culture, using aseptic technique and knowledge of medium components and cell requirements. Conduct medical research under direction of microbiologist or biochemist. Harvest cell cultures at optimum time based on knowledge of cell cycle differences and culture conditions.

Hottest Field Where They Work—Health Care.

Work Conditions—Indoors; contaminants; disease or infections; hazardous conditions; using hands on objects, tools, or controls; repetitive motions.

Educational Programs—Cytotechnology/Cytotechnologist; Clinical Laboratory Science/Medical Technology/Technologist; Histologic Technology/ Histotechnologist; Cytogenetics/Genetics/Clinical Genetics Technology/ Technologist; Renal/Dialysis Technologist/Technician; Clinical/Medical Laboratory Science and Allied Professions, Other.

Network Systems and Data Communications Analysts

- Level of Education/Training: Bachelor's degree
- Annual Earnings: $61,750
- Growth: 54.6%
- Annual Job Openings: 43,000
- Personality Type: Investigative (IR)

Evening or weekend work may be necessary to meet deadlines or solve specific problems. With the technology available today, telecommuting is common for computer professionals.

On the Job—Analyze, design, test, and evaluate network systems, such as local area networks (LAN), wide area networks (WAN), Internet, intranet, and other data communications systems. Perform network modeling, analysis, and planning. Research and recommend network and data communications hardware and software. Includes telecommunications specialists who deal with the interfacing of computer and communications equipment. May supervise computer programmers. Maintain needed files by adding and deleting files on the network server and backing up files to guarantee their safety in the event of problems with the network. Monitor system performance and provide security measures, troubleshooting, and maintenance as needed. Assist users to diagnose and solve data communication problems. Set up user accounts, regulating and monitoring file access to ensure confidentiality and proper use. Design and implement systems, network configurations, and network architecture, including hardware and software technology, site locations, and integration of technologies. Maintain the peripherals, such as printers, that are connected to the network. Identify areas of operation that need upgraded equipment such as modems, fiber-optic cables, and telephone wires. Train users in use of equipment. Develop and write procedures for installation, use, and troubleshooting of communications hardware and software. Adapt and modify existing software to meet specific needs. Work with other engineers, systems analysts, programmers, technicians, scientists, and top-level managers in the design, testing, and evaluation of systems. Test and evaluate hardware and software to determine efficiency, reliability, and compatibility with existing system and make purchase recommendations. Read technical manuals and brochures to determine which equipment meets establishment requirements. Consult customers, visit workplaces, or conduct surveys to determine present and future user needs. Visit vendors, attend conferences or training, and study technical journals to keep up with changes in technology.

Hottest Fields Where They Work—Computer Systems Design and Related Services; Management, Scientific, and Technical Consulting Services; Internet Service Providers, Web Search Portals, and Data Processing Services; State and Local Government, Excluding Education and Hospitals; Educational Services.

Work Conditions—Indoors; sitting.

Educational Programs—Computer and Information Sciences, General; Information Technology; Computer Systems Analysis/Analyst; Computer Systems Networking and Telecommunications; System, Networking, and LAN/WAN Management/Manager; Computer and Information Systems Security.

Physician Assistants

- Level of Education/Training: Bachelor's degree
- Annual Earnings: $72,030
- Growth: 49.6%
- Annual Job Openings: 10,000
- Personality Type: Investigative (IS)

All states require physician assistants to pass a national exam in order to obtain a license.

On the Job—Provide health care services typically performed by a physician under the supervision of a physician. Conduct complete physicals, provide treatment, and counsel patients. May, in some cases, prescribe medication. Must graduate from an accredited educational program for physician assistants. Examine patients to obtain information about their physical condition. Make tentative diagnoses and decisions about management and treatment of patients. Interpret diagnostic test results for deviations from normal. Obtain, compile, and record patient medical data, including health history, progress notes, and results of physical examination. Administer or order diagnostic tests, such as X-ray, electrocardiogram, and laboratory tests. Prescribe therapy or medication with physician approval. Perform therapeutic procedures, such as injections, immunizations, suturing and wound care, and infection management. Instruct and counsel patients about prescribed therapeutic regimens, normal growth and development, family planning, emotional problems of daily living, and health maintenance. Provide physicians with assistance during surgery or complicated medical procedures. Supervise and coordinate activities of technicians and technical assistants. Visit and observe patients on hospital rounds or house calls, updating charts, ordering therapy, and reporting back to physician. Order medical and laboratory supplies and equipment.

Hottest Field Where They Work—Health Care.

Work Conditions—Indoors; disease or infections; standing.

Educational Program—Physician Assistant.

Artistic Jobs Requiring Short-Term On-the-Job Training

Costume Attendants

- Level of Education/Training: Short-term on-the-job training
- Annual Earnings: $25,360
- Growth: 23.4%
- Annual Job Openings: 2,000
- Personality Type: Artistic (ARS)

Job openings tend to be found where there are stage shows, such as in theaters, at casinos, and on cruise ships.

On the Job—Select, fit, and take care of costumes for cast members and aid entertainers. Distribute costumes and related equipment and keep records of item status. Arrange costumes in order of use to facilitate quick-change procedures for performances. Return borrowed or rented items when productions are complete and return other items to storage. Clean and press costumes before and after performances and perform any minor repairs. Assign lockers to employees and maintain locker rooms, dressing rooms, wig rooms, and costume storage and laundry areas. Provide assistance to cast members in wearing costumes or assign cast dressers to assist specific cast members with costume changes. Design and construct costumes or send them to tailors for construction, major repairs, or alterations. Purchase, rent, or requisition costumes and other wardrobe necessities. Check the appearance of costumes on stage and under lights to determine whether desired effects are being achieved. Inventory stock to determine types and conditions of available costuming. Collaborate with production designers, costume designers, and other production staff to discuss and execute costume design details. Monitor, maintain, and secure inventories of costumes, wigs, and makeup, providing keys or access to assigned directors, costume designers, and wardrobe mistresses/masters. Create worksheets for dressing lists, show notes, and costume checks. Direct the work of wardrobe crews during dress rehearsals and performances. Examine costume fit on cast members and sketch or write notes for alterations. Review scripts or other production information to determine a story's locale and period, as well as the number of characters and required costumes. Recommend vendors and monitor their work. Study books, pictures, and examples of period clothing to determine styles worn during specific periods in history. Provide managers with budget recommendations and take responsibility for budgetary line items related to costumes, storage, and makeup needs. Participate in the hiring, training, scheduling, and supervision of alteration workers. Care for non-clothing items such as flags, table skirts, and draperies.

Hottest Fields Where They Work—Arts, Entertainment, and Recreation; Hotels and Other Accommodations; Educational Services.

Work Conditions—Indoors; contaminants; standing; walking and running; using hands on objects, tools, or controls.

Artistic Jobs Requiring a Bachelor's Degree

Technical Writers

- Level of Education/Training: Bachelor's degree
- Annual Earnings: $55,160

- Growth: 23.2%
- Annual Job Openings: 5,000
- Personality Type: Artistic (AI)

Rapid growth and change in the high-technology and electronics industries result in a greater need for people to write users' guides, instruction manuals, and training materials. This work requires people who not only are technically skilled as writers, but also are familiar with the subject area.

On the Job—Write technical materials, such as equipment manuals, appendices, or operating and maintenance instructions. May assist in layout work. Organize material and complete writing assignment according to set standards regarding order, clarity, conciseness, style, and terminology. Maintain records and files of work and revisions. Edit, standardize, or make changes to material prepared by other writers or establishment personnel. Confer with customer representatives, vendors, plant executives, or publisher to establish technical specifications and to determine subject material to be developed for publication. Review published materials and recommend revisions or changes in scope, format, content, and methods of reproduction and binding. Select photographs, drawings, sketches, diagrams, and charts to illustrate material. Study drawings, specifications, mockups, and product samples to integrate and delineate technology, operating procedure, and production sequence and detail. Interview production and engineering personnel and read journals and other material to become familiar with product technologies and production methods. Observe production, developmental, and experimental activities to determine operating procedure and detail. Arrange for typing, duplication, and distribution of material. Assist in laying out material for publication. Analyze developments in specific field to determine need for revisions in previously published materials and development of new material. Review manufacturer's and trade catalogs, drawings, and other data relative to operation, maintenance, and service of equipment. Draw sketches to illustrate specified materials or assembly sequence.

Hottest Fields Where They Work—Computer Systems Design and Related Services; Software Publishers; Management, Scientific, and Technical Consulting Services; Employment Services; Internet Service Providers, Web Search Portals, and Data Processing Services.

Work Conditions—Indoors; sitting; using hands on objects, tools, or controls; repetitive motions.

Educational Programs—Communication Studies/Speech Communication and Rhetoric; Technical and Business Writing; Business/Corporate Communications.

Social Jobs Requiring Short-Term On-the-Job Training

Nursing Aides, Orderlies, and Attendants

- Level of Education/Training: Short-term on-the-job training
- Annual Earnings: $21,440
- Growth: 22.3%
- Annual Job Openings: 307,000
- Personality Type: Social (SR)

Most jobs are in nursing and residential care facilities, hospitals, and home health care services.

On the Job—Provide basic patient care under direction of nursing staff. Perform duties such as feeding, bathing, dressing, grooming, or moving patients or changing linens. Turn and reposition bedridden patients, alone or with assistance, to prevent bedsores. Answer patients' call signals. Feed patients who are unable to feed themselves. Observe patients' conditions, measuring and recording food and liquid intake and output and vital signs, and report changes to professional staff. Provide patient care by supplying and emptying bedpans, applying dressings, and supervising exercise routines. Provide patients with help walking, exercising, and moving in and out of bed. Bathe, groom, shave, dress, or drape patients to prepare them for surgery, treatment, or examination. Collect specimens such as urine, feces, or sputum. Prepare, serve, and collect food trays. Clean rooms and change linens. Transport patients to treatment units, using a wheelchair or stretcher. Deliver messages, documents, and specimens. Answer phones and direct visitors. Administer medications and treatments, such as catheterizations, suppositories, irrigations, enemas, massages, and douches, as directed by a physician or nurse. Restrain patients if necessary. Maintain inventory by storing, preparing, sterilizing, and issuing supplies such as dressing packs and treatment trays. Explain medical instructions to patients and family members. Perform clerical duties such as processing documents and scheduling appointments. Work as part of a medical team that examines and treats clinic outpatients. Set up equipment such as oxygen tents, portable X-ray machines, and overhead irrigation bottles.

Hottest Fields Where They Work—Health Care; Employment Services.

Work Conditions—Indoors; disease or infections; standing; walking and running; using hands on objects, tools, or controls; bending or twisting the body.

Physical Therapist Aides

- Level of Education/Training: Short-term on-the-job training
- Annual Earnings: $21,510
- Growth: 34.4%
- Annual Job Openings: 5,000
- Personality Type: Social (SR)

Physical therapist aides usually learn skills on the job. They may face keen competition from the large pool of qualified applicants.

On the Job—Under close supervision of a physical therapist or physical therapy assistant, perform only delegated, selected, or routine tasks in specific situations. These duties include preparing the patient and the treatment area. Clean and organize work area and disinfect equipment after treatment. Observe patients during treatment to compile and evaluate data on patients' responses and progress and report to physical therapist. Instruct, motivate, safeguard, and assist patients practicing exercises and functional activities under direction of medical staff. Secure patients into or onto therapy equipment. Transport patients to and from treatment areas, using wheelchairs or providing standing support. Confer with physical therapy staff or others to discuss and evaluate patient information for planning, modifying, and coordinating treatment. Record treatment given and equipment used. Perform clerical duties, such as taking inventory, ordering supplies, answering telephone, taking messages, and filling out forms. Maintain equipment and furniture to keep it in good working condition, including performing the assembly and disassembly of equipment and accessories. Administer active and passive manual therapeutic exercises; therapeutic massage; and heat, light, sound, water, or electrical modality treatments, such as ultrasound. Change linens, such as bedsheets and pillowcases. Arrange treatment supplies to keep them in order. Assist patients to dress; undress; and put on and remove supportive devices, such as braces, splints, and slings. Measure patient's range of joint motion, body parts, and vital signs to determine effects of treatments or for patient evaluations. Fit patients for orthopedic braces, prostheses, or supportive devices, adjusting fit as needed, and train patients to use them. Participate in patient care tasks, such as assisting with passing food trays, feeding residents, or bathing residents on bed rest. Administer traction to relieve neck and back pain, using intermittent and static traction equipment.

Hottest Field Where They Work—Health Care.

Work Conditions—Indoors; disease or infections; standing; walking and running; using hands on objects, tools, or controls; repetitive motions.

Security Guards

- Level of Education/Training: Short-term on-the-job training
- Annual Earnings: $20,760
- Growth: 12.6%
- Annual Job Openings: 230,000
- Personality Type: Social (SEC)

Competition is expected for higher-paying positions at facilities requiring longer periods of training and a high level of security, such as nuclear power plants and weapons installations.

On the Job—Guard, patrol, or monitor premises to prevent theft, violence, or infractions of rules. Patrol industrial or commercial premises to prevent and detect signs of intrusion and ensure security of doors, windows, and gates. Answer alarms and investigate disturbances. Monitor and authorize entrance and departure of employees, visitors, and other persons to guard against theft and maintain security of premises. Write reports of daily activities and irregularities such as equipment or property damage, theft, presence of unauthorized persons, or unusual occurrences. Call police or fire departments in cases of emergency, such as fire or presence of unauthorized persons. Circulate among visitors, patrons, or employees to preserve order and protect property. Answer telephone calls to take messages, answer questions, and provide information during non-business hours or when switchboard is closed. Warn persons of rule infractions or violations and apprehend or evict violators from premises, using force when necessary. Operate detecting devices to screen individuals and prevent passage of prohibited articles into restricted areas. Escort or drive motor vehicle to transport individuals to specified locations or to provide personal protection. Inspect and adjust security systems, equipment, or machinery to ensure operational use and to detect evidence of tampering. Drive or guard armored vehicle to transport money and valuables to prevent theft and ensure safe delivery. Monitor and adjust controls that regulate building systems, such as air conditioning, furnace, or boiler.

Hottest Fields Where They Work—Employment Services; Arts, Entertainment, and Recreation; Management, Scientific, and Technical Consulting Services.

Work Conditions—More often outdoors than indoors; noisy; very hot or cold; more often sitting than standing.

Teacher Assistants

- Level of Education/Training: Short-term on-the-job training
- Annual Earnings: $20,090

- Growth: 14.1%
- Annual Job Openings: 252,000
- Personality Type: Social (SC)

About 4 in 10 teacher assistants work part time.

On the Job—Perform duties that are instructional in nature or deliver direct services to students or parents. Serve in a position for which a teacher or another professional has ultimate responsibility for the design and implementation of educational programs and services. Provide extra assistance to students with special needs, such as non–English-speaking students or those with physical and mental disabilities. Tutor and assist children individually or in small groups to help them master assignments and to reinforce learning concepts presented by teachers. Supervise students in classrooms, halls, cafeterias, schoolyards, and gymnasiums or on field trips. Enforce administration policies and rules governing students. Observe students' performance and record relevant data to assess progress. Discuss assigned duties with classroom teachers in order to coordinate instructional efforts. Instruct and monitor students in the use and care of equipment and materials to prevent injuries and damage. Present subject matter to students under the direction and guidance of teachers, using lectures, discussions, or supervised role-playing methods. Organize and label materials and display students' work in a manner appropriate for their eye levels and perceptual skills. Distribute tests and homework assignments and collect them when they are completed. Type, file, and duplicate materials. Distribute teaching materials such as textbooks, workbooks, papers, and pencils to students. Use computers, audiovisual aids, and other equipment and materials to supplement presentations. Attend staff meetings and serve on committees as required. Prepare lesson materials, bulletin board displays, exhibits, equipment, and demonstrations. Carry out therapeutic regimens such as behavior modification and personal development programs under the supervision of special education instructors, psychologists, or speech-language pathologists. Provide disabled students with assistive devices, supportive technology, and assistance accessing facilities such as restrooms. Assist in bus loading and unloading. Take class attendance and maintain attendance records. Grade homework and tests and compute and record results, using answer sheets or electronic marking devices. Organize and supervise games and other recreational activities to promote physical, mental, and social development.

Hottest Fields Where They Work—Educational Services; Child Day Care Services.

Work Conditions—Indoors; noisy; standing.

Social Jobs Requiring Moderate-Term On-the-Job Training

Animal Trainers

- Level of Education/Training: Moderate-term on-the-job training
- Annual Earnings: $24,800
- Growth: 20.3%
- Annual Job Openings: 3,000
- Personality Type: Social (SRE)

About 3 in 5 animal trainers were self-employed.

On the Job—**Train animals for riding, harness, security, performance, or obedience or for assisting persons with disabilities. Accustom animals to human voice and contact and condition animals to respond to commands. Train animals according to prescribed standards for show or competition. May train animals to carry pack loads or work as part of pack team.** Observe animals' physical conditions to detect illness or unhealthy conditions requiring medical care. Cue or signal animals during performances. Administer prescribed medications to animals. Evaluate animals to determine their temperaments, abilities, and aptitude for training. Feed and exercise animals and provide other general care such as cleaning and maintaining holding and performance areas. Talk to and interact with animals to familiarize them to human voices and contact. Conduct training programs to develop and maintain desired animal behaviors for competition, entertainment, obedience, security, riding, and related areas. Keep records documenting animal health, diet, and behavior. Advise animal owners regarding the purchase of specific animals. Instruct jockeys in handling specific horses during races. Train horses or other equines for riding, harness, show, racing, or other work, using knowledge of breed characteristics, training methods, performance standards, and the peculiarities of each animal. Use oral, spur, rein, and hand commands to condition horses to carry riders or to pull horse-drawn equipment. Place tack or harnesses on horses to accustom horses to the feel of equipment. Train dogs in human-assistance or property protection duties. Retrain horses to break bad habits, such as kicking, bolting, and resisting bridling and grooming. Train and rehearse animals, according to scripts, for motion picture, television, film, stage, or circus performances. Organize and conduct animal shows. Arrange for mating of stallions and mares and assist mares during foaling.

Hottest Fields Where They Work—Agriculture, Forestry, and Fishing; Arts, Entertainment, and Recreation.

Work Conditions—Outdoors; noisy; standing; walking and running; using hands on objects, tools, or controls; repetitive motions.

Dental Assistants

- Level of Education/Training: Moderate-term on-the-job training
- Annual Earnings: $29,520
- Growth: 42.7%
- Annual Job Openings: 45,000
- Personality Type: Social (SR)

Most assistants learn their skills on the job, although an increasing number are trained in dental-assisting programs; most programs take 1 year or less to complete.

On the Job—**Assist dentist, set up patient and equipment, and keep records.** Prepare patient, sterilize and disinfect instruments, set up instrument trays, prepare materials, and assist dentist during dental procedures. Expose dental diagnostic X rays. Record treatment information in patient records. Take and record medical and dental histories and vital signs of patients. Provide postoperative instructions prescribed by dentist. Assist dentist in management of medical and dental emergencies. Pour, trim, and polish study casts. Instruct patients in oral hygiene and plaque control programs. Make preliminary impressions for study casts and occlusal registrations for mounting study casts. Clean and polish removable appliances. Clean teeth, using dental instruments. Apply protective coating of fluoride to teeth. Fabricate temporary restorations and custom impressions from preliminary impressions. Schedule appointments, prepare bills and receive payment for dental services, complete insurance forms, and maintain records manually or by using computer.

Hottest Field Where They Work—Health Care.

Work Conditions—Indoors; contaminants; disease or infections; using hands on objects, tools, or controls; bending or twisting the body; repetitive motions.

Medical Assistants

- Level of Education/Training: Moderate-term on-the-job training
- Annual Earnings: $25,350
- Growth: 52.1%
- Annual Job Openings: 93,000
- Personality Type: Social (SC)

Job prospects should be best for medical assistants with formal training or experience, particularly those with certification.

On the Job—Perform administrative and certain clinical duties under the direction of physician. Administrative duties may include scheduling appointments, maintaining medical records, billing, and coding for insurance purposes. Clinical duties may include taking and recording vital signs and medical histories, preparing patients for examination, drawing blood, and administering medications as directed by physician. Interview patients to obtain medical information and measure their vital signs, weight, and height. Show patients to examination rooms and prepare them for the physician. Record patients' medical history, vital statistics, and information such as test results in medical records. Prepare and administer medications as directed by a physician. Collect blood, tissue, or other laboratory specimens; log the specimens; and prepare them for testing. Explain treatment procedures, medications, diets, and physicians' instructions to patients. Help physicians examine and treat patients, handing them instruments and materials or performing such tasks as giving injections or removing sutures. Authorize drug refills and provide prescription information to pharmacies. Prepare treatment rooms for patient examinations, keeping the rooms neat and clean. Clean and sterilize instruments and dispose of contaminated supplies. Schedule appointments for patients. Change dressings on wounds. Greet and log in patients arriving at office or clinic. Contact medical facilities or departments to schedule patients for tests or admission. Perform general office duties such as answering telephones, taking dictation, or completing insurance forms. Inventory and order medical, lab, or office supplies and equipment. Perform routine laboratory tests and sample analyses. Set up medical laboratory equipment. Keep financial records and perform other bookkeeping duties, such as handling credit and collections and mailing monthly statements to patients. Operate X-ray, electrocardiogram (EKG), and other equipment to administer routine diagnostic tests. Give physiotherapy treatments such as diathermy, galvanics, and hydrotherapy.

Hottest Field Where They Work—Health Care.

Work Conditions—Indoors; disease or infections; standing; walking and running; using hands on objects, tools, or controls.

Residential Advisors

- Level of Education/Training: Moderate-term on-the-job training
- Annual Earnings: $21,850
- Growth: 28.9%
- Annual Job Openings: 22,000
- Personality Type: Social (SC)

Many employers prefer applicants who have a high school education and either directly related experience or college-level coursework in counseling, social work, education, or a closely related field of study.

On the Job—Coordinate activities for residents of boarding schools, college fraternities or sororities, college dormitories, or similar establishments. Order supplies and determine need for maintenance, repairs, and furnishings. May maintain household records and assign rooms. May refer residents to counseling resources if needed. Enforce rules and regulations to ensure the smooth and orderly operation of dormitory programs. Provide emergency first aid and summon medical assistance when necessary. Mediate interpersonal problems between residents. Administer, coordinate, or recommend disciplinary and corrective actions. Communicate with other staff to resolve problems with individual students. Counsel students in the handling of issues such as family, financial, and educational problems. Make regular rounds to ensure that residents and areas are safe and secure. Observe students to detect and report unusual behavior. Determine the need for facility maintenance and repair and notify appropriate personnel. Collaborate with counselors to develop counseling programs that address the needs of individual students. Develop program plans for individuals or assist in plan development. Hold regular meetings with each assigned unit. Direct and participate in on- and off-campus recreational activities for residents of institutions, boarding schools, fraternities or sororities, children's homes, or similar establishments. Assign rooms to students. Provide requested information on students' progress and the development of case plans. Confer with medical personnel to better understand the backgrounds and needs of individual residents. Answer telephones and route calls or deliver messages. Supervise participants in work-study programs. Process contract cancellations for students who are unable to follow residence hall policies and procedures. Sort and distribute mail. Supervise the activities of housekeeping personnel. Order supplies for facilities. Supervise students' housekeeping work to ensure that it is done properly. Chaperone group-sponsored trips and social functions. Compile information such as residents' daily activities and the quantities of supplies used to prepare required reports. Accompany and supervise students during meals. Provide transportation or escort for expeditions such as shopping trips or visits to doctors or dentists. Inventory, pack, and remove items left behind by former residents.

Hottest Fields Where They Work—Health Care; Educational Services; Social Assistance, Except Child Day Care.

Work Conditions—Indoors; noisy; sitting.

Social and Human Service Assistants

- Level of Education/Training: Moderate-term on-the-job training
- Annual Earnings: $25,030

- Growth: 29.7%
- Annual Job Openings: 61,000
- Personality Type: Social (SC)

While a bachelor's degree usually is not required, employers increasingly seek individuals with relevant work experience or education beyond high school.

On the Job—Assist professionals from a wide variety of fields, such as psychology, rehabilitation, or social work, to provide client services, as well as support for families. May assist clients in identifying available benefits and social and community services and help clients obtain them. May assist social workers with developing, organizing, and conducting programs to prevent and resolve problems relevant to substance abuse, human relationships, rehabilitation, or adult daycare. Provide information and refer individuals to public or private agencies or community services for assistance. Keep records and prepare reports for owner or management concerning visits with clients. Visit individuals in homes or attend group meetings to provide information on agency services, requirements, and procedures. Advise clients regarding food stamps, child care, food, money management, sanitation, or housekeeping. Submit reports and review reports or problems with superior. Oversee day-to-day group activities of residents in institution. Interview individuals and family members to compile information on social, educational, criminal, institutional, or drug history. Meet with youth groups to acquaint them with consequences of delinquent acts. Transport and accompany clients to shopping areas or to appointments, using automobile. Explain rules established by owner or management, such as sanitation and maintenance requirements and parking regulations. Observe and discuss meal preparation and suggest alternate methods of food preparation. Demonstrate use and care of equipment for tenant use. Consult with supervisor concerning programs for individual families. Monitor free, supplementary meal program to ensure cleanliness of facility and that eligibility guidelines are met for persons receiving meals. Observe clients' food selections and recommend alternate economical and nutritional food choices. Inform tenants of facilities such as laundries and playgrounds. Care for children in client's home during client's appointments. Assist in locating housing for displaced individuals. Assist clients with preparation of forms, such as tax or rent forms. Assist in planning of food budget, using charts and sample budgets.

Hottest Fields Where They Work—Social Assistance, Except Child Day Care; Health Care; Advocacy, Grantmaking, and Civic Organizations; State and Local Government, Excluding Education and Hospitals.

Work Conditions—Indoors; noisy; sitting.

Social Jobs Requiring Work Experience in a Related Occupation

Self-Enrichment Education Teachers

- Level of Education/Training: Work experience in a related occupation
- Annual Earnings: $32,360
- Growth: 25.3%
- Annual Job Openings: 74,000
- Personality Type: Social (SA)

Part-time jobs, a lack of benefits, and self-employed workers are relatively common among self-enrichment teachers.

On the Job—Teach or instruct courses other than those that normally lead to an occupational objective or degree. Courses may include self-improvement, nonvocational, and nonacademic subjects. Teaching may or may not take place in a traditional educational institution. Adapt teaching methods and instructional materials to meet students' varying needs and interests. Conduct classes, workshops, and demonstrations and provide individual instruction to teach topics and skills such as cooking, dancing, writing, physical fitness, photography, personal finance, and flying. Monitor students' performance in order to make suggestions for improvement and to ensure that they satisfy course standards, training requirements, and objectives. Observe students to determine qualifications, limitations, abilities, interests, and other individual characteristics. Instruct students individually and in groups, using various teaching methods such as lectures, discussions, and demonstrations. Establish clear objectives for all lessons, units, and projects and communicate those objectives to students. Instruct and monitor students in use and care of equipment and materials to prevent injury and damage. Prepare students for further development by encouraging them to explore learning opportunities and to persevere with challenging tasks. Prepare materials and classrooms for class activities. Enforce policies and rules governing students. Plan and conduct activities for a balanced program of instruction, demonstration, and work time that provides students with opportunities to observe, question, and investigate. Prepare instructional program objectives, outlines, and lesson plans. Maintain accurate and complete student records as required by administrative policy. Participate in publicity planning and student recruitment. Plan and supervise class projects, field trips, visits by guest speakers, contests, or other experiential activities and guide students in learning from those activities. Attend professional meetings, conferences, and workshops to maintain and improve professional competence. Meet with other instructors to discuss individual students and their progress.

Confer with other teachers and professionals to plan and schedule lessons promoting learning and development. Attend staff meetings and serve on committees as required. Prepare and administer written, oral, and performance tests and issue grades in accordance with performance.

Hottest Fields Where They Work—Educational Services; Arts, Entertainment, and Recreation; Social Assistance, Except Child Day Care.

Work Conditions—Indoors; standing.

Vocational Education Teachers, Postsecondary

- Level of Education/Training: Work experience in a related occupation
- Annual Earnings: $41,750
- Growth: 32.2%
- Annual Job Openings: 329,000
- Personality Type: Social (SR)

The job openings listed here are shared with 35 other postsecondary teaching occupations.

> In general, teachers need a bachelor's or higher degree, plus at least 3 years of work experience in their field. In some fields, a license or certificate that demonstrates one's qualifications may be all that is required.

On the Job—Teach or instruct vocational or occupational subjects at the postsecondary level (but at less than the baccalaureate) to students who have graduated or left high school. Includes correspondence school instructors; industrial, commercial, and government training instructors; and adult education teachers and instructors who prepare persons to operate industrial machinery and equipment and transportation and communications equipment. Teaching may take place in public or private schools whose primary business is education or in a school associated with an organization whose primary business is other than education. Supervise and monitor students' use of tools and equipment. Observe and evaluate students' work to determine progress, provide feedback, and make suggestions for improvement. Present lectures and conduct discussions to increase students' knowledge and competence, using visual aids such as graphs, charts, videotapes, and slides. Administer oral, written, or performance tests to measure progress and to evaluate training effectiveness. Prepare reports and maintain records such as student grades, attendance rolls, and training activity details. Supervise independent or group projects, field placements, laboratory work, or other training. Determine training needs of students or workers. Provide individualized instruction and tutorial or remedial instruction. Conduct on-the-job training, classes, or training sessions to teach and demonstrate principles, techniques, procedures, or methods of designated subjects. Develop curricula and plan course content and methods of instruction. Prepare outlines of instructional programs and training schedules and establish course goals. Integrate academic and vocational curricula so that students can obtain a variety of skills. Develop teaching aids such as instructional software, multimedia visual aids, or study materials. Select and assemble books, materials, supplies, and equipment for training, courses, or projects. Advise students on course selection, career decisions, and other academic and vocational concerns. Participate in conferences, seminars, and training sessions to keep abreast of developments in the field and integrate relevant information into training programs. Serve on faculty and school committees concerned with budgeting, curriculum revision, and course and diploma requirements. Review enrollment applications and correspond with applicants to obtain additional information. Arrange for lectures by experts in designated fields.

Hottest Field Where They Work—Educational Services.

Work Conditions—Indoors; standing; using hands on objects, tools, or controls.

Social Jobs Requiring Postsecondary Vocational Training

Emergency Medical Technicians and Paramedics

- Level of Education/Training: Postsecondary vocational training
- Annual Earnings: $26,080
- Growth: 27.3%
- Annual Job Openings: 21,000
- Personality Type: Social (SRI)

Competition will be greater for jobs in local fire, police, and rescue squad departments than in private ambulance services; opportunities will be best for those who have advanced certification.

On the Job—Assess injuries, administer emergency medical care, and extricate trapped individuals. Transport injured or sick persons to medical facilities. Administer first-aid treatment and life-support care to sick or injured persons in prehospital setting. Operate equipment such as electrocardiograms (EKGs), external defibrillators, and bag-valve mask resuscitators in advanced life-support environments. Assess nature and extent of illness or injury to establish and prioritize medical procedures. Maintain vehicles and medical and communication equipment and replenish first-aid equipment and supplies. Observe, record, and report to physician the patient's condition or injury, the treatment provided, and reactions to drugs and treatment. Perform emergency diagnostic and treatment procedures, such as stomach suction, airway management, or heart monitoring, during ambulance ride. Administer drugs, orally or by injection, and perform intravenous procedures under a physician's direction. Comfort and reassure patients. Coordinate work with other emergency medical team members and police and fire department personnel. Communicate with dispatchers and treatment center personnel to provide information about situation, to arrange reception of victims, and to receive instructions for further treatment. Immobilize patient for placement on stretcher and ambulance transport, using backboard or other spinal immobilization device. Decontaminate ambulance interior following treatment of patient with infectious disease and report case to proper authorities. Drive mobile intensive care unit to specified location, following instructions from emergency medical dispatcher. Coordinate with treatment center personnel to obtain patients' vital statistics and medical history, to determine the circumstances of the emergency, and to administer emergency treatment.

Hottest Fields Where They Work—Health Care; State and Local Government, Excluding Education and Hospitals.

Work Conditions—Outdoors; noisy; very bright or dim lighting; contaminants; cramped work space, awkward positions; disease or infections.

Educational Programs—Emergency Care Attendant (EMT Ambulance); Emergency Medical Technology/Technician (EMT Paramedic).

Fitness Trainers and Aerobics Instructors

- Level of Education/Training: Postsecondary vocational training
- Annual Earnings: $25,840
- Growth: 27.1%
- Annual Job Openings: 50,000
- Personality Type: Social (SRE)

Persons planning for these careers should be outgoing, good at motivating people, and sensitive to the needs of others. Excellent health and physical fitness are typically required.

On the Job—Instruct or coach groups or individuals in exercise activities and the fundamentals of sports. Demonstrate techniques and methods of participation.

Observe participants and inform them of corrective measures necessary to improve their skills. Those required to hold teaching degrees should be reported in the appropriate teaching category. Explain and enforce safety rules and regulations governing sports, recreational activities, and the use of exercise equipment. Offer alternatives during classes to accommodate different levels of fitness. Plan routines, choose appropriate music, and choose different movements for each set of muscles, depending on participants' capabilities and limitations. Observe participants and inform them of corrective measures necessary for skill improvement. Teach proper breathing techniques used during physical exertion. Teach and demonstrate use of gymnastic and training equipment such as trampolines and weights. Instruct participants in maintaining exertion levels to maximize benefits from exercise routines. Maintain fitness equipment. Conduct therapeutic, recreational, or athletic activities. Monitor participants' progress and adapt programs as needed. Evaluate individuals' abilities, needs, and physical conditions and develop suitable training programs to meet any special requirements. Plan physical education programs to promote development of participants' physical attributes and social skills. Provide students with information and resources regarding nutrition, weight control, and lifestyle issues. Administer emergency first aid, wrap injuries, treat minor chronic disabilities, or refer injured persons to physicians. Advise clients about proper clothing and shoes. Wrap ankles, fingers, wrists, or other body parts with synthetic skin, gauze, or adhesive tape to support muscles and ligaments. Teach individual and team sports to participants through instruction and demonstration, utilizing knowledge of sports techniques and of participants' physical capabilities. Promote health clubs through membership sales and record member information. Organize, lead, and referee indoor and outdoor games such as volleyball, baseball, and basketball. Maintain equipment inventories and select, store, or issue equipment as needed. Organize and conduct competitions and tournaments. Advise participants in use of heat or ultraviolet treatments and hot baths. Massage body parts to relieve soreness, strains, and bruises.

Hottest Fields Where They Work—Arts, Entertainment, and Recreation; Educational Services; Health Care; Advocacy, Grantmaking, and Civic Organizations.

Work Conditions—Indoors; standing; walking and running; repetitive motions.

Educational Programs—Physical Education Teaching and Coaching; Health and Physical Education, General; Sport and Fitness Administration/Management.

Preschool Teachers, Except Special Education

- Level of Education/Training: Postsecondary vocational training
- Annual Earnings: $21,990
- Growth: 33.1%

- Annual Job Openings: 77,000
- Personality Type: Social (SA)

Preschool teachers working in day care settings often work year round. Part-time schedules are common.

On the Job—Instruct children (normally up to 5 years of age) in activities designed to promote social, physical, and intellectual growth needed for primary school in preschool, day care center, or other child development facility. May be required to hold state certification. Provide a variety of materials and resources for children to explore, manipulate, and use, both in learning activities and in imaginative play. Attend to children's basic needs by feeding them, dressing them, and changing their diapers. Establish and enforce rules for behavior and procedures for maintaining order. Read books to entire classes or to small groups. Teach basic skills such as color, shape, number and letter recognition, personal hygiene, and social skills. Organize and lead activities designed to promote physical, mental, and social development, such as games, arts and crafts, music, storytelling, and field trips. Observe and evaluate children's performance, behavior, social development, and physical health. Meet with parents and guardians to discuss their children's progress and needs, determine their priorities for their children, and suggest ways that they can promote learning and development. Identify children showing signs of emotional, developmental, or health-related problems and discuss them with supervisors, parents or guardians, and child development specialists. Enforce all administration policies and rules governing students. Prepare materials and classrooms for class activities. Serve meals and snacks in accordance with nutritional guidelines. Teach proper eating habits and personal hygiene. Assimilate arriving children to the school environment by greeting them, helping them remove outerwear, and selecting activities of interest to them. Adapt teaching methods and instructional materials to meet students' varying needs and interests. Establish clear objectives for all lessons, units, and projects and communicate those objectives to children. Demonstrate activities to children. Arrange indoor and outdoor space to facilitate creative play, motor-skill activities, and safety. Plan and conduct activities for a balanced program of instruction, demonstration, and work time that provides students with opportunities to observe, question, and investigate. Maintain accurate and complete student records as required by laws, district policies, and administrative regulations.

Hottest Fields Where They Work—Child Day Care Services; Educational Services.

Work Conditions—Indoors; standing; walking and running; bending or twisting the body.

Educational Programs—Montessori Teacher Education; Early Childhood Education and Teaching; Child Care and Support Services Management.

Social Jobs Requiring an Associate Degree

Dental Hygienists

- Level of Education/Training: Associate degree
- Annual Earnings: $60,890
- Growth: 43.3%
- Annual Job Openings: 17,000
- Personality Type: Social (SC)

More than half work part time, and flexible scheduling is a distinctive feature of this job.

On the Job—Clean teeth and examine oral areas, head, and neck for signs of oral disease. May educate patients on oral hygiene, take and develop X rays, or apply fluoride or sealants. Clean calcareous deposits, accretions, and stains from teeth and beneath margins of gums, using dental instruments. Feel and visually examine gums for sores and signs of disease. Chart conditions of decay and disease for diagnosis and treatment by dentist. Feel lymph nodes under patient's chin to detect swelling or tenderness that could indicate presence of oral cancer. Apply fluorides and other cavity-preventing agents to arrest dental decay. Examine gums, using probes, to locate periodontal recessed gums and signs of gum disease. Expose and develop X-ray film. Provide clinical services and health education to improve and maintain oral health of schoolchildren. Remove excess cement from coronal surfaces of teeth. Make impressions for study casts. Place, carve, and finish amalgam restorations. Administer local anesthetic agents. Conduct dental health clinics for community groups to augment services of dentist. Remove sutures and dressings. Place and remove rubber dams, matrices, and temporary restorations.

Hottest Field Where They Work—Health Care.

Work Conditions—Indoors; radiation; disease or infections; sitting; using hands on objects, tools, or controls; repetitive motions.

Educational Program—Dental Hygiene/Hygienist.

Occupational Therapist Assistants

- Level of Education/Training: Associate degree
- Annual Earnings: $39,750
- Growth: 34.1%

- Annual Job Openings: 2,000
- Personality Type: Social (SR)

In an effort to control rising health care costs, third-party payers are expected to encourage occupational therapists to delegate more hands-on therapy work to occupational therapist assistants.

On the Job—Assist occupational therapists in providing occupational therapy treatments and procedures. May, in accordance with state laws, assist in development of treatment plans, carry out routine functions, direct activity programs, and document the progress of treatments. Generally requires formal training. Observe and record patients' progress, attitudes, and behavior and maintain this information in client records. Maintain and promote a positive attitude toward clients and their treatment programs. Monitor patients' performance in therapy activities, providing encouragement. Select therapy activities to fit patients' needs and capabilities. Instruct, or assist in instructing, patients and families in home programs, basic living skills, and the care and use of adaptive equipment. Evaluate the daily living skills and capacities of physically, developmentally, or emotionally disabled clients. Aid patients in dressing and grooming themselves. Implement, or assist occupational therapists with implementing, treatment plans designed to help clients function independently. Report to supervisors, verbally or in writing, on patients' progress, attitudes, and behavior. Alter treatment programs to obtain better results if treatment is not having the intended effect. Work under the direction of occupational therapists to plan, implement, and administer educational, vocational, and recreational programs that restore and enhance performance in individuals with functional impairments. Design, fabricate, and repair assistive devices and make adaptive changes to equipment and environments. Assemble, clean, and maintain equipment and materials for patient use. Teach patients how to deal constructively with their emotions. Perform clerical duties such as scheduling appointments, collecting data, and documenting health insurance billings. Transport patients to and from the occupational therapy work area. Demonstrate therapy techniques such as manual and creative arts or games. Order any needed educational or treatment supplies. Assist educational specialists or clinical psychologists in administering situational or diagnostic tests to measure client's abilities or progress.

Hottest Field Where They Work—Health Care.

Work Conditions—Indoors; disease or infections; standing; walking and running; using hands on objects, tools, or controls; bending or twisting the body.

Educational Program—Occupational Therapist Assistant.

Physical Therapist Assistants

- Level of Education/Training: Associate degree
- Annual Earnings: $39,490
- Growth: 44.2%
- Annual Job Openings: 7,000
- Personality Type: Social (SR)

About 60 percent of jobs are in hospitals or offices of physical therapists.

On the Job—Assist physical therapists in providing physical therapy treatments and procedures. May, in accordance with state laws, assist in the development of treatment plans, carry out routine functions, document the progress of treatment, and modify specific treatments in accordance with patient status and within the scope of treatment plans established by a physical therapist. Generally requires formal training. Instruct, motivate, safeguard, and assist patients as they practice exercises and functional activities. Confer with physical therapy staff or others to discuss and evaluate patient information for planning, modifying, and coordinating treatment. Administer active and passive manual therapeutic exercises; therapeutic massage; and heat, light, sound, water, and electrical modality treatments, such as ultrasound. Observe patients during treatments to compile and evaluate data on patients' responses and progress and report to physical therapist. Measure patients' range of joint motion, body parts, and vital signs to determine effects of treatments or for patient evaluations. Secure patients into or onto therapy equipment. Fit patients for orthopedic braces, prostheses, and supportive devices such as crutches and train them in their use. Transport patients to and from treatment areas, lifting and transferring them according to positioning requirements. Monitor operation of equipment and record use of equipment and administration of treatment. Clean work area and check and store equipment after treatment. Assist patients to dress; undress; or put on and remove supportive devices, such as braces, splints, and slings. Administer traction to relieve neck and back pain, using intermittent and static traction equipment. Perform clerical duties, such as taking inventory, ordering supplies, answering telephone, taking messages, and filling out forms. Prepare treatment areas and electrotherapy equipment for use by physiotherapists. Perform postural drainage, percussions, and vibrations and teach deep breathing exercises to treat respiratory conditions.

Hottest Field Where They Work—Health Care.

Work Conditions—Indoors; disease or infections; standing; walking and running; using hands on objects, tools, or controls; bending or twisting the body.

Educational Program—Physical Therapist Assistant.

Radiation Therapists

- Level of Education/Training: Associate degree
- Annual Earnings: $62,340
- Growth: 26.3%
- Annual Job Openings: 1,000
- Personality Type: Social (SRI)

Good job opportunities are expected; applicants who are certified and who possess a bachelor's or an associate degree or a certificate in radiation therapy should have the best prospects.

On the Job—Provide radiation therapy to patients as prescribed by a radiologist according to established practices and standards. Duties may include reviewing prescription and diagnosis; acting as liaison with physician and supportive care personnel; preparing equipment, such as immobilization, treatment, and protection devices; and maintaining records, reports, and files. May assist in dosimetry procedures and tumor localization. Administer prescribed doses of radiation to specific body parts, using radiation therapy equipment according to established practices and standards. Position patients for treatment with accuracy according to prescription. Enter data into computer and set controls to operate and adjust equipment and regulate dosage. Follow principles of radiation protection for patient, self, and others. Maintain records, reports, and files as required, including such information as radiation dosages, equipment settings, and patients' reactions. Review prescription, diagnosis, patient chart, and identification. Conduct most treatment sessions independently in accordance with the long-term treatment plan and under the general direction of the patient's physician. Check radiation therapy equipment to ensure proper operation. Observe and reassure patients during treatment and report unusual reactions to physician or turn equipment off if unexpected adverse reactions occur. Check for side effects such as skin irritation, nausea, and hair loss to assess patients' reaction to treatment. Educate, prepare, and reassure patients and their families by answering questions, providing physical assistance, and reinforcing physicians' advice regarding treatment reactions and post-treatment care. Calculate actual treatment dosages delivered during each session. Prepare and construct equipment, such as immobilization, treatment, and protection devices. Photograph treated area of patient and process film. Help physicians, radiation oncologists, and clinical physicists to prepare physical and technical aspects of radiation treatment plans, using information about patient condition and anatomy. Train and supervise student or subordinate radiotherapy technologists. Provide assistance to other health care personnel during dosimetry procedures and tumor localization. Implement appropriate follow-up care plans. Act as liaison with physicist and supportive care personnel. Store, sterilize, or prepare the special applicators containing the radioactive substance implanted by the physician. Assist in the preparation of sealed radioactive materials, such as cobalt, radium, cesium, and isotopes, for use in radiation treatments.

Hottest Field Where They Work—Health Care.

Work Conditions—Indoors; disease or infections; standing; walking and running; using hands on objects, tools, or controls; repetitive motions.

Educational Program—Medical Radiologic Technology/Science—Radiation Therapist.

Registered Nurses

- Level of Education/Training: Associate degree
- Annual Earnings: $54,670
- Growth: 29.4%
- Annual Job Openings: 229,000
- Personality Type: Social (SI)

Individuals considering nursing should carefully weigh the advantages and disadvantages of enrolling in a bachelor's program because if they do, their advancement opportunities usually are broader. In fact, some career paths are open only to nurses with a bachelor's or master's degree.

On the Job—Assess patient health problems and needs, develop and implement nursing care plans, and maintain medical records. Administer nursing care to ill, injured, convalescent, or disabled patients. May advise patients on health maintenance and disease prevention or provide case management. Licensing or registration required. Includes advance practice nurses such as nurse practitioners, clinical nurse specialists, certified nurse midwives, and certified registered nurse anesthetists. Advanced practice nursing is practiced by RNs who have specialized formal, post-basic education and who function in highly autonomous and specialized roles. Maintain accurate, detailed reports and records. Monitor, record, and report symptoms and changes in patients' conditions. Record patients' medical information and vital signs. Modify patient treatment plans as indicated by patients' responses and conditions. Consult and coordinate with health care team members to assess, plan, implement, and evaluate patient care plans. Order, interpret, and evaluate diagnostic tests to identify and assess patient's condition. Monitor all aspects of patient care, including diet and physical activity. Direct and supervise less-skilled nursing or health care personnel or supervise a particular unit. Prepare patients for, and assist with, examinations and treatments. Observe nurses and visit patients to ensure proper nursing care. Assess the needs of individuals, families, or communities, including assessment of individuals' home or work environments, to identify potential health or safety problems. Instruct individuals, families, and other groups on topics such as health education, disease prevention, and childbirth and develop health improvement programs. Prepare rooms, sterile instruments, equipment, and supplies and ensure that stock of supplies is maintained. Inform physician of patient's condition during anesthesia. Deliver infants and provide prenatal and postpartum care and treatment under obstetrician's supervision. Administer local, inhalation, intravenous, and other anesthetics. Provide health care, first aid, immunizations, and assistance in convalescence and rehabilitation in locations such as schools, hospitals, and industry. Conduct specified laboratory tests. Perform physical examinations, make tentative diagnoses, and treat patients en route to hospitals or at disaster site triage centers. Hand items to surgeons during operations. Prescribe or recommend drugs, medical devices, or other forms of treatment, such as physical therapy, inhalation therapy, or related therapeutic procedures. Direct and coordinate infection control programs, advising and consulting with specified personnel about necessary precautions. Perform administrative and managerial functions, such as taking responsibility for a unit's staff, budget, planning, and long-range goals.

Hottest Field Where They Work—Health Care.

Work Conditions—Indoors; noisy; contaminants; disease or infections; standing; using hands on objects, tools, or controls.

Educational Programs—Nursing—Registered Nurse Training (RN, ASN, BSN, MSN); Adult Health Nurse/Nursing; Nurse Anesthetist; Family Practice Nurse/ Nurse Practitioner; Maternal/Child Health and Neonatal Nurse/Nursing; Nurse Midwife/Nursing Midwifery; Nursing Science (MS, PhD); Pediatric Nurse/ Nursing; Psychiatric/Mental Health Nurse/Nursing; Public Health/Community Nurse/Nursing; others.

Social Jobs Requiring a Bachelor's Degree

Athletic Trainers

- Level of Education/Training: Bachelor's degree
- Annual Earnings: $34,260
- Growth: 29.3%
- Annual Job Openings: 1,000
- Personality Type: Social (SR)

Some states require that you complete an internship in addition to a college degree.

On the Job—Evaluate, advise, and treat athletes to assist recovery from injury, avoid injury, or maintain peak physical fitness. Conduct an initial assessment of an athlete's injury or illness to provide emergency or continued care and to determine whether they should be referred to physicians for definitive diagnosis and treatment. Care for athletic injuries, using physical therapy equipment, techniques, and medication. Evaluate athletes' readiness to play and provide participation clearances when necessary and warranted. Apply protective or injury-preventive devices such as tape, bandages, or braces to body parts such as ankles, fingers, or wrists. Assess and report the progress of recovering athletes to coaches and physicians. Collaborate with physicians to develop and implement comprehensive rehabilitation programs for athletic injuries. Advise athletes on the proper use of equipment. Plan and implement comprehensive athletic injury and illness prevention programs. Develop training programs and routines designed to improve athletic performance. Travel with athletic teams to be available at sporting events. Instruct coaches, athletes, parents, medical personnel, and community members in the care and prevention of athletic injuries. Inspect playing fields to locate any items that could injure players. Conduct research and provide instruction on subject matter related to athletic training or sports medicine. Recommend special diets to improve athletes' health, increase their stamina, or alter their weight. Massage body parts to relieve soreness, strains, and bruises. Confer with coaches to select protective equipment. Accompany injured athletes to hospitals. Perform team-support duties such as running errands, maintaining equipment, and stocking supplies. Lead stretching exercises for team members prior to games and practices.

Hottest Fields Where They Work—Health Care; Arts, Entertainment, and Recreation; Educational Services.

Work Conditions—More often indoors than outdoors; very hot or cold; contaminants; disease or infections; standing.

Educational Program—Athletic Training/Trainer.

Elementary School Teachers, Except Special Education

- Level of Education/Training: Bachelor's degree
- Annual Earnings: $44,040
- Growth: 18.2%
- Annual Job Openings: 203,000
- Personality Type: Social (SAI)

Job prospects should be better in inner cities and rural areas than in suburban districts.

On the Job—Teach pupils in public or private schools at the elementary level basic academic, social, and other formative skills. Establish and enforce rules for behavior and procedures for maintaining order among the students for whom they are responsible. Observe and evaluate students' performance, behavior, social development, and physical health. Prepare materials and classrooms for class activities. Adapt teaching methods and instructional materials to meet students' varying needs and interests. Plan and conduct activities for a balanced program of instruction, demonstration, and work time that provides students with opportunities to observe, question, and investigate. Instruct students individually and in groups, using various teaching methods such as lectures, discussions, and demonstrations. Establish clear objectives for all lessons, units, and projects and communicate those objectives to students. Assign and grade class work and homework. Read books to entire classes or small groups. Prepare, administer, and grade tests and assignments to evaluate students' progress. Confer with parents or guardians, teachers, counselors, and administrators to resolve students' behavioral and academic problems. Meet with parents and guardians to discuss their children's progress and to determine their priorities for their children and their resource needs. Prepare students for later grades by encouraging them to explore learning opportunities and to persevere with challenging tasks. Maintain accurate and complete student records as required by laws, district policies, and administrative regulations. Guide and counsel students with adjustment or academic problems or special academic interests. Prepare and implement remedial programs for students requiring extra help. Prepare objectives and outlines for courses of study, following curriculum guidelines or requirements of states and schools. Provide a variety of materials and resources for children to explore, manipulate, and use, both in learning activities and in imaginative play. Enforce administration policies and rules governing students. Confer with other staff members to plan and schedule lessons promoting learning, following approved curricula.

Hottest Field Where They Work—Educational Services.

Work Conditions—Indoors; noisy; disease or infections; standing.

Educational Programs—Elementary Education and Teaching; Teacher Education, Multiple Levels; Montessori Teacher Education.

Employment Interviewers

- Level of Education/Training: Bachelor's degree
- Annual Earnings: $41,780
- Growth: 30.5%
- Annual Job Openings: 30,000
- Personality Type: Social (SEC)

The job openings listed here are shared with Personnel Recruiters.

In filling entry-level jobs, many employers seek college graduates who have majored in human resources, human resources administration, or industrial and labor relations. Other employers look for college graduates with a technical or business background or a well-rounded liberal arts education.

On the Job—Interview job applicants in employment office and refer them to prospective employers for consideration. Search application files, notify selected applicants of job openings, and refer qualified applicants to prospective employers. Contact employers to verify referral results. Record and evaluate various pertinent data. Inform applicants of job openings and details such as duties and responsibilities, compensation, benefits, schedules, working conditions, and promotion opportunities. Interview job applicants to match their qualifications with employers' needs, recording and evaluating applicant experience, education, training, and skills. Review employment applications and job orders to match applicants with job requirements, using manual or computerized file searches. Select qualified applicants or refer them to employers according to organization policy. Perform reference and background checks on applicants. Maintain records of applicants not selected for employment. Instruct job applicants in presenting a positive image by providing help with resume writing, personal appearance, and interview techniques. Refer applicants to services such as vocational counseling, literacy or language instruction, transportation assistance, vocational training, and child care. Contact employers to solicit orders for job vacancies, determining their requirements and recording relevant data such as job descriptions. Conduct workshops and demonstrate the use of job listings to assist applicants with skill building. Search for and recruit applicants for open positions through campus job fairs and advertisements. Provide background information on organizations with which interviews are scheduled. Administer assessment tests to identify skill-building needs. Conduct or arrange for skill, intelligence, or psychological testing of applicants and current employees. Hire workers and place them with employers needing temporary help. Evaluate selection and testing techniques by conducting research or follow-up activities and conferring with management and supervisory personnel.

Hottest Fields Where They Work—Employment Services; Management, Scientific, and Technical Consulting Services; Social Assistance, Except Child Day Care; State and Local Government, Excluding Education and Hospitals; Educational Services.

Work Conditions—Indoors; sitting; repetitive motions.

Educational Programs—Human Resources Management/Personnel Administration, General; Labor and Industrial Relations.

Kindergarten Teachers, Except Special Education

- Level of Education/Training: Bachelor's degree
- Annual Earnings: $42,230
- Growth: 22.4%
- Annual Job Openings: 28,000
- Personality Type: Social (SA)

You may want to attain professional certification to demonstrate competency beyond that required for a license.

On the Job—Teach elemental, natural, and social science; personal hygiene; music; art; and literature to children from 4 to 6 years old. Promote physical, mental, and social development. May be required to hold state certification. Teach basic skills such as color, shape, number and letter recognition, personal hygiene, and social skills. Establish and enforce rules for behavior and policies and procedures to maintain order among students. Observe and evaluate children's performance, behavior, social development, and physical health. Instruct students individually and in groups, adapting teaching methods to meet students' varying needs and interests. Read books to entire classes or to small groups. Demonstrate activities to children. Provide a variety of materials and resources for children to explore, manipulate, and use, both in learning activities and in imaginative play. Plan and conduct activities for a balanced program of instruction, demonstration, and work time that provides students with opportunities to observe, question, and investigate. Confer with parents or guardians, other teachers, counselors, and administrators to resolve students' behavioral and academic problems. Prepare children for later grades by encouraging them to explore learning opportunities and to persevere with challenging tasks. Establish clear objectives for all lessons, units, and projects and communicate those objectives to children. Prepare and implement remedial programs for students requiring extra help. Meet with parents and guardians to discuss their children's progress and to determine their priorities for their children and their resource needs. Prepare objectives and outlines for courses of study, following curriculum guidelines or requirements of states and schools. Organize and lead activities designed to promote physical, mental, and social development such as games, arts and crafts, music, and storytelling. Guide and counsel students with adjustment or academic problems or special academic interests. Identify children showing signs of emotional, developmental, or health-related problems and discuss them with supervisors, parents or guardians, and child development specialists. Instruct and monitor students in the use and care of equipment and materials to prevent injuries and damage. Assimilate arriving children to the school environment by greeting them, helping them remove outerwear, and selecting activities of interest to them.

125

Hottest Fields Where They Work—Educational Services; Child Day Care Services.

Work Conditions—Indoors; disease or infections; standing.

Educational Programs—Montessori Teacher Education; Waldorf/Steiner Teacher Education; Kindergarten/Preschool Education and Teaching; Early Childhood Education and Teaching.

Medical and Public Health Social Workers

- Level of Education/Training: Bachelor's degree
- Annual Earnings: $41,120
- Growth: 25.9%
- Annual Job Openings: 14,000
- Personality Type: Social (SI)

While a bachelor's degree is the minimum requirement, a master's degree in social work or a related field has become the standard for many positions.

On the Job—**Provide persons, families, or vulnerable populations with the psychosocial support needed to cope with chronic, acute, or terminal illnesses, such as Alzheimer's, cancer, or AIDS. Services include advising family caregivers, providing patient education and counseling, and making necessary referrals for other social services.** Collaborate with other professionals to evaluate patients' medical or physical condition and to assess client needs. Investigate child abuse or neglect cases and take authorized protective action when necessary. Refer patient, client, or family to community resources to assist in recovery from mental or physical illness and to provide access to services such as financial assistance, legal aid, housing, job placement, or education. Counsel clients and patients in individual and group sessions to help them overcome dependencies, recover from illness, and adjust to life. Organize support groups or counsel family members to assist them in understanding, dealing with, and supporting the client or patient. Advocate for clients or patients to resolve crises. Identify environmental impediments to client or patient progress through interviews and review of patient records. Utilize consultation data and social work experience to plan and coordinate client or patient care and rehabilitation, following through to ensure service efficacy. Modify treatment plans to comply with changes in clients' status. Monitor, evaluate, and record client progress according to measurable goals described in treatment and care plan. Supervise and direct other workers providing services to clients or patients. Develop or advise on social policy and assist in community development.

Oversee Medicaid- and Medicare-related paperwork and recordkeeping in hospitals. Conduct social research to advance knowledge in the social work field. Plan and conduct programs to combat social problems, prevent substance abuse, or improve community health and counseling services.

Hottest Fields Where They Work—Health Care; Social Assistance, Except Child Day Care; State and Local Government, Excluding Education and Hospitals.

Work Conditions—Indoors; noisy; disease or infections; sitting.

Educational Program—Clinical/Medical Social Work.

Personal Financial Advisors

- Level of Education/Training: Bachelor's degree
- Annual Earnings: $63,500
- Growth: 25.9%
- Annual Job Openings: 17,000
- Personality Type: Social (SEC)

The best opportunities exist for those who have certification, which usually requires relevant experience, 2 to 3 years of study beyond the bachelor's, passing a comprehensive examination, and adherence to an enforceable code of ethics.

On the Job—Advise clients on financial plans, utilizing knowledge of tax and investment strategies, securities, insurance, pension plans, and real estate. Duties include assessing clients' assets, liabilities, cash flow, insurance coverage, tax status, and financial objectives to establish investment strategies. Open accounts for clients and disburse funds from account to creditors as agents for clients. Research and investigate available investment opportunities to determine whether they fit into financial plans. Recommend strategies clients can use to achieve their financial goals and objectives, including specific recommendations in such areas as cash management, insurance coverage, and investment planning. Sell financial products such as stocks, bonds, mutual funds, and insurance if licensed to do so. Collect information from students to determine their eligibility for specific financial aid programs. Conduct seminars and workshops on financial planning topics such as retirement planning, estate planning, and the evaluation of severance packages. Contact clients' creditors to arrange for payment adjustments so that payments are feasible for clients and agreeable to creditors. Meet with clients' other advisors, including attorneys, accountants, trust officers, and investment bankers, to fully understand clients' financial goals and circumstances. Authorize release of financial aid funds to students. Participate in the selection of candidates for specific financial aid awards. Determine amounts of aid to be granted to students, considering such factors as funds available, extent of demand, and financial needs. Build and maintain client bases, keeping current client plans up to date and recruiting new clients on an ongoing basis. Review clients' accounts and plans regularly to determine whether life changes, economic changes, or financial performance indicate a need for plan reassessment. Prepare and interpret for clients information such as investment performance reports, financial document summaries, and income projections. Answer clients' questions about the purposes and details of financial plans and strategies. Contact clients periodically to determine if there have been changes in their financial status. Devise debt liquidation plans that include payoff priorities and timelines. Explain and document for clients the types of services that are to be provided and the responsibilities to be taken by the personal financial advisor.

Hottest Fields Where They Work—Securities, Commodities, and Other Investments; Insurance.

Work Conditions—Indoors; sitting.

Educational Programs—Finance, General; Financial Planning and Services.

Secondary School Teachers, Except Special and Vocational Education

- Level of Education/Training: Bachelor's degree
- Annual Earnings: $46,060
- Growth: 14.4%
- Annual Job Openings: 107,000
- Personality Type: Social (SAI)

Currently, many school districts have difficulty hiring qualified teachers in some subject areas—most often mathematics, science (especially chemistry and physics), bilingual education, and foreign languages.

On the Job—Instruct students in secondary public or private schools in one or more subjects at the secondary level, such as English, mathematics, or social studies. May be designated according to subject matter specialty, such as typing instructors, commercial teachers, or English teachers. Establish and enforce rules for behavior and procedures for maintaining order among the students for whom they are responsible. Instruct through lectures, discussions, and demonstrations in one or more subjects such as English, mathematics, or social studies. Establish clear objectives for all lessons, units, and projects and communicate those objectives to students. Prepare, administer, and grade tests and assignments to evaluate students' progress. Prepare materials and classrooms for class activities. Adapt teaching methods and instructional materials to meet students' varying needs and interests. Assign and grade class work and homework. Maintain accurate and complete student records as required by laws, district policies, and administrative regulations. Enforce all administration policies and rules governing students. Observe and evaluate students' performance, behavior, social development, and physical health. Plan and conduct activities for a balanced program of instruction, demonstration, and work time that provides students with opportunities to observe, question, and investigate. Prepare students for later grades by encouraging them to explore learning opportunities and to persevere with challenging tasks. Guide and counsel students with adjustment or academic problems or special academic interests. Instruct and monitor students in the use and care of equipment and materials to prevent injuries and damage. Prepare for assigned classes and show written evidence of preparation upon request of immediate supervisors. Meet with parents and guardians to discuss their children's progress and to determine their priorities for their children and their resource needs. Confer with parents or guardians, other teachers, counselors, and administrators to resolve students' behavioral and academic problems. Use computers, audiovisual aids, and other equipment and materials to supplement presentations. Prepare objectives and outlines for courses of study, following curriculum guidelines or requirements of states and schools. Meet with other professionals to discuss individual students' needs and progress.

Hottest Field Where They Work—Educational Services.

Work Conditions—Indoors; noisy; standing.

Educational Programs—Junior High/Intermediate/Middle School Education and Teaching; Secondary Education and Teaching; Teacher Education, Multiple Levels; Waldorf/Steiner Teacher Education; Agricultural Teacher Education; Art Teacher Education; Business Teacher Education; Driver and Safety Teacher Education; English/Language Arts Teacher Education; Foreign Language Teacher Education; Health Teacher Education; others.

Social and Community Service Managers

- Level of Education/Training: Bachelor's degree
- Annual Earnings: $49,500
- Growth: 25.5%
- Annual Job Openings: 17,000
- Personality Type: Social (SE)

An internship while in college can be extremely valuable for gaining experience in this field.

On the Job—Plan, organize, or coordinate the activities of a social service program or community outreach organization. **Oversee the program or organization's budget and policies regarding participant involvement, program requirements, and benefits. Work may involve directing social workers, counselors, or probation officers.** Establish and maintain relationships with other agencies and organizations in community to meet community needs and to ensure that services are not duplicated. Prepare and maintain records and reports such as budgets, personnel records, or training manuals. Direct activities of professional and technical staff and volunteers. Evaluate the work of staff and volunteers to ensure that programs are of appropriate quality and that resources are used effectively. Establish and oversee administrative procedures to meet objectives set by boards of directors or senior management. Participate in the determination of organizational policies regarding such issues as participant eligibility, program requirements, and program benefits. Research and analyze member or community needs to determine program directions and goals. Speak to community groups to explain and interpret agency purposes, programs, and policies. Recruit, interview, and hire or sign up volunteers and staff. Represent organizations in relations with governmental and media institutions. Plan and administer budgets for programs, equipment, and support services. Analyze proposed legislation, regulations, or rule changes to determine how agency services could be impacted. Act as consultants to agency staff and other community programs regarding the interpretation of program-related federal, state, and county regulations and policies. Implement and evaluate staff training programs. Direct fundraising activities and the preparation of public relations materials.

Hottest Fields Where They Work—Social Assistance, Except Child Day Care; Health Care; Advocacy, Grantmaking, and Civic Organizations; State and Local Government, Excluding Education and Hospitals.

Work Conditions—Indoors; noisy; sitting.

Educational Programs—Human Services, General; Community Organization and Advocacy; Public Administration; Business/Commerce, General; Business Administration and Management, General; Non-Profit/Public/Organizational Management; Entrepreneurship/Entrepreneurial Studies; Business, Management, Marketing, and Related Support Services, Other.

Special Education Teachers, Middle School

- Level of Education/Training: Bachelor's degree
- Annual Earnings: $45,490
- Growth: 19.9%
- Annual Job Openings: 8,000
- Personality Type: Social (SA)

Many states are offering alternative licensure programs to attract people to these jobs who do not have the qualifications to become teachers under normal procedures.

On the Job—Teach middle school subjects to educationally and physically handicapped students. Includes teachers who specialize and work with audibly and visually handicapped students and those who teach basic academic and life processes skills to the mentally impaired. Establish and enforce rules for behavior and policies and procedures to maintain order among students. Maintain accurate and complete student records and prepare reports on children and activities as required by laws, district policies, and administrative regulations. Prepare materials and classrooms for class activities. Confer with parents, administrators, testing specialists, social workers, and professionals to develop individual educational plans designed to promote students' educational, physical, and social development. Develop and implement strategies to meet the needs of students with a variety of handicapping conditions. Teach socially acceptable behavior, employing techniques such as behavior modification and positive reinforcement. Modify the general education curriculum for special-needs students based upon a variety of instructional techniques and instructional technology. Employ special educational strategies and techniques during instruction to improve the development of sensory- and perceptual-motor skills, language, cognition, and memory. Confer with parents or guardians, other teachers, counselors, and administrators in order to resolve students' behavioral and academic problems. Instruct through lectures, discussions, and demonstrations in one or more subjects such as English, mathematics, or social studies. Coordinate placement of students with special needs into mainstream classes. Meet with parents and guardians to discuss their children's progress and to determine their priorities for their children and their resource needs. Guide and counsel students with adjustment or academic problems or special academic interests. Prepare, administer, and grade tests and assignments to evaluate students' progress. Observe and evaluate students' performance, behavior, social development, and physical health. Establish clear objectives for all lessons, units, and projects and communicate those objectives to students. Teach students personal development skills such as goal setting, independence, and self-advocacy. Plan and conduct activities for a balanced program of instruction, demonstration, and work time that provides students with opportunities to observe, question, and investigate.

Hottest Field Where They Work—Educational Services.

Work Conditions—Indoors; noisy; standing.

Educational Programs—Special Education and Teaching, General; Education/ Teaching of the Gifted and Talented; Education/Teaching of Individuals Who Are Developmentally Delayed; Education/Teaching of Individuals in Early Childhood Special Education Programs.

Special Education Teachers, Preschool, Kindergarten, and Elementary School

- Level of Education/Training: Bachelor's degree
- Annual Earnings: $44,630
- Growth: 23.3%
- Annual Job Openings: 18,000
- Personality Type: Social (SA)

Excellent job prospects are expected due to rising enrollments of special education students and reported shortages of qualified teachers.

On the Job—Teach elementary and preschool school subjects to educationally and physically handicapped students. Includes teachers who specialize and work with audibly and visually handicapped students and those who teach basic academic and life processes skills to the mentally impaired. Instruct students in academic subjects, using a variety of techniques such as phonetics, multisensory learning, and repetition, in order to reinforce learning and to meet students' varying needs and interests. Employ special educational strategies and techniques during instruction to improve the development of sensory- and perceptual-motor skills, language, cognition, and memory. Teach socially acceptable behavior, employing techniques such as behavior modification and positive reinforcement. Modify the general education curriculum for special-needs students based upon a variety of instructional techniques and technologies. Meet with parents and guardians to discuss their children's progress and to determine their priorities for their children and their resource needs. Plan and conduct activities for a balanced program of instruction, demonstration, and work time that provides students with opportunities to observe, question, and investigate. Establish and enforce rules for behavior and policies and procedures to maintain order among the students for whom they are responsible. Confer with parents, administrators, testing specialists, social workers, and professionals to develop individual educational plans designed to promote students' educational, physical, and social development. Maintain accurate and complete student records and prepare reports on children and activities as required by laws, district policies, and administrative regulations. Establish clear objectives for all lessons, units, and projects and communicate those objectives to students. Develop and implement strategies to meet the needs of students with a variety of handicapping conditions. Prepare classrooms for class activities and provide a variety of materials and resources for children to explore, manipulate, and use, both in learning activities and imaginative play. Confer with parents or guardians, teachers, counselors, and administrators in order to resolve students' behavioral and academic problems. Observe and evaluate students' performance, behavior, social development, and physical health. Teach students personal development skills such as goal setting, independence, and self-advocacy.

Hottest Field Where They Work—Educational Services.

Work Conditions—Indoors; noisy; standing.

Educational Programs—Special Education and Teaching, General; Education/Teaching of Individuals with Hearing Impairments, Including Deafness; Education/Teaching of the Gifted and Talented; Education/Teaching of Individuals with Emotional Disturbances; Education/Teaching of Individuals with Mental Retardation; Education/Teaching of Individuals with Multiple Disabilities; Education/Teaching of Individuals with Orthopedic and Other Physical Health Impairments; others.

Training and Development Specialists

- Level of Education/Training: Bachelor's degree
- Annual Earnings: $45,870
- Growth: 20.8%
- Annual Job Openings: 32,000
- Personality Type: Social (SEC)

A range of personal qualities and skills is necessary, including the ability to speak and write effectively. The growing diversity of the workforce requires working with or supervising people with various cultural backgrounds, levels of education, and experience.

On the Job—Conduct training and development programs for employees. Keep up with developments in area of expertise by reading current journals, books, and magazine articles. Present information, using a variety of instructional techniques and formats such as role playing, simulations, team exercises, group discussions, videos, and lectures. Schedule classes based on availability of classrooms, equipment, and instructors. Organize and develop, or obtain, training procedure manuals and guides and course materials such as handouts and visual materials. Offer specific training programs to help workers maintain or improve job skills. Monitor, evaluate, and record training activities and program effectiveness. Attend meetings and seminars to obtain information for use in training programs or to inform management of training program status. Coordinate recruitment and placement of training program participants. Evaluate training materials prepared by instructors, such as outlines, text, and handouts. Develop alternative training methods if expected improvements are not seen. Assess training needs through surveys; interviews with employees; focus groups; or consultation with managers, instructors, or customer representatives. Screen, hire, and assign workers to positions based on qualifications. Select and assign instructors to conduct training. Devise programs to develop executive potential among employees in lower-level positions. Design, plan, organize, and direct orientation and training for employees or customers of industrial or commercial establishment. Negotiate contracts with clients, including desired training outcomes, fees, and expenses. Supervise instructors, evaluate instructor performance, and refer instructors to classes for skill development. Monitor training costs to ensure budget is not exceeded and prepare budget reports to justify expenditures. Refer trainees to employer relations representatives, to locations offering job placement assistance, or to appropriate social services agencies if warranted.

Hottest Fields Where They Work—Health Care; Educational Services; Management, Scientific, and Technical Consulting Services; Social Assistance, Except Child Day Care; Employment Services.

Work Conditions—Indoors; noisy; standing; repetitive motions.

Educational Programs—Human Resources Management/Personnel Administration, General; Organizational Behavior Studies.

Enterprising Jobs Requiring Moderate-Term On-the-Job Training

Sales Representatives, Wholesale and Manufacturing, Except Technical and Scientific Products

- Level of Education/Training: Moderate-term on-the-job training
- Annual Earnings: $47,380
- Growth: 12.9%
- Annual Job Openings: 169,000
- Personality Type: Enterprising (ES)

Employment opportunities will be best for those with a college degree, the appropriate knowledge or technical expertise, and the personal traits necessary for successful selling.

On the Job—Sell goods for wholesalers or manufacturers to businesses or groups of individuals. Work requires substantial knowledge of items sold. Answer customers' questions about products, prices, availability, product uses, and credit terms. Recommend products to customers based on customers' needs and interests. Contact regular and prospective customers to demonstrate products, explain product features, and solicit orders. Estimate or quote prices, credit or contract terms, warranties, and delivery dates. Consult with clients after sales or contract signings to resolve problems and to provide ongoing support. Prepare drawings, estimates, and bids that meet specific customer needs. Provide customers with product samples and catalogs. Identify prospective customers by using business directories, following leads from existing clients, participating in organizations and clubs, and attending trade shows and conferences. Arrange and direct delivery and installation of products and equipment. Monitor market conditions; product innovations; and competitors' products, prices, and sales. Negotiate details of contracts and payments and prepare sales contracts and order forms. Perform administrative duties, such as preparing sales budgets and reports, keeping sales records, and filing expense account reports. Obtain credit information about prospective customers. Forward orders to manufacturers. Check stock levels and reorder merchandise as necessary. Plan, assemble, and stock product displays in retail stores or make recommendations to retailers regarding product displays, promotional programs, and advertising. Negotiate with retail merchants to improve product exposure such as shelf positioning and advertising. Train customers' employees to operate and maintain new equipment. Buy products from manufacturers or brokerage firms and distribute them to wholesale and retail clients.

Hottest Field Where They Work—Wholesale Trade.

Work Conditions—Outdoors; noisy; contaminants; more often standing than sitting; walking and running.

Enterprising Jobs Requiring Long-Term On-the-Job Training

Athletes and Sports Competitors

- Level of Education/Training: Long-term on-the-job training
- Annual Earnings: $39,930
- Growth: 21.1%
- Annual Job Openings: 6,000
- Personality Type: Enterprising (ERS)

Competition for professional athlete jobs will continue to be extremely intense; athletes who seek to compete professionally must have extraordinary talent, desire, and dedication to training.

On the Job—Compete in athletic events. Lead teams by serving as captains. Receive instructions from coaches and other sports staff prior to events and discuss their performance afterwards. Participate in athletic events and competitive sports according to established rules and regulations. Maintain optimum physical fitness levels by training regularly, following nutrition plans, and consulting with health professionals. Exercise and practice under the direction of athletic trainers or professional coaches in order to develop skills, improve physical condition, and prepare for competitions. Attend scheduled practice and training sessions. Assess performance following athletic competition, identifying strengths and weaknesses and making adjustments to improve future performance. Maintain equipment used in a particular sport. Represent teams or professional sports clubs, performing such activities as meeting with members of the media, making speeches, or participating in charity events.

Hottest Field Where They Work—Arts, Entertainment, and Recreation.

Work Conditions—More often outdoors than indoors; minor burns, cuts, bites, or stings; standing; walking and running; bending or twisting the body.

Coaches and Scouts

- Level of Education/Training: Long-term on-the-job training
- Annual Earnings: $25,990
- Growth: 20.4%
- Annual Job Openings: 63,000
- Personality Type: Enterprising (ERS)

Job opportunities will be best for part-time coaches. Full-time coaches usually work more than 40 hours a week for several months during the sports season, if not most of the year.

On the Job—Instruct or coach groups or individuals in the fundamentals of sports. Demonstrate techniques and methods of participation. May evaluate athletes' strengths and weaknesses as possible recruits or to improve the athletes' technique to prepare them for competition. Those required to hold teaching degrees should be reported in the appropriate teaching category. Plan, organize, and conduct practice sessions. Provide training direction, encouragement, and motivation in order to prepare athletes for games, competitive events, and tours. Identify and recruit potential athletes, arranging and offering incentives such as athletic scholarships. Plan strategies and choose team members for individual games or sports seasons. Plan and direct physical conditioning programs that will enable athletes to achieve maximum performance. Adjust coaching techniques based on the strengths and weaknesses of athletes. File scouting reports that detail player assessments, provide recommendations on athlete recruitment, and identify locations and individuals to be targeted for future recruitment efforts. Keep records of athlete, team, and opposing team performance. Instruct individuals or groups in sports rules; game strategies; and performance principles such as specific ways of moving the body, hands, or feet in order to achieve desired results. Analyze the strengths and weaknesses of opposing teams in order to develop game strategies. Evaluate athletes' skills and review performance records in order to determine their fitness and potential in a particular area of athletics. Keep abreast of changing rules, techniques, technologies, and philosophies relevant to their sport. Monitor athletes' use of equipment in order to ensure safe and proper use. Explain and enforce safety rules and regulations. Develop and arrange competition schedules and programs. Serve as organizer, leader, instructor, or referee for outdoor and indoor games, such as volleyball, football, and soccer. Explain and demonstrate the use of sports and training equipment, such as trampolines or weights. Perform activities that support a team or a specific sport, such as meeting with media representatives and appearing at fundraising events. Arrange and conduct sports-related activities such as training camps, skill-improvement courses, clinics, and pre-season try-outs. Select, acquire, store, and issue equipment and other materials as necessary. Negotiate with professional athletes or their representatives in order to obtain services and arrange contracts.

Hottest Fields Where They Work—Educational Services; Arts, Entertainment, and Recreation.

Work Conditions—More often indoors than outdoors; noisy; standing; walking and running.

Enterprising Jobs Requiring Work Experience in a Related Occupation

First-Line Supervisors/Managers of Food Preparation and Serving Workers

- Level of Education/Training: Work experience in a related occupation
- Annual Earnings: $26,050
- Growth: 16.6%
- Annual Job Openings: 187,000
- Personality Type: Enterprising (ERC)

Experience in the food preparation and services industry, whether as a cook, a waiter or waitress, or a counter attendant, is essential training.

On the Job—Supervise workers engaged in preparing and serving food. Compile and balance cash receipts at the end of the day or shift. Resolve customer complaints regarding food service. Inspect supplies, equipment, and work areas to ensure efficient service and conformance to standards. Train workers in food preparation and in service, sanitation, and safety procedures. Control inventories of food, equipment, smallware, and liquor and report shortages to designated personnel. Observe and evaluate workers and work procedures in order to ensure quality standards and service. Assign duties, responsibilities, and workstations to employees in accordance with work requirements. Estimate ingredients and supplies required to prepare a recipe. Perform personnel actions such as hiring and firing staff, consulting with other managers as necessary. Analyze operational problems, such as theft and waste, and establish procedures to alleviate these problems. Specify food portions and courses, production and time sequences, and workstation and equipment arrangements. Recommend measures for improving work procedures and worker performance to increase service quality and enhance job safety. Greet and seat guests and present menus and wine lists. Present bills and accept payments. Forecast staff, equipment, and supply requirements based on a master menu. Record production and operational data on specified forms. Perform serving duties such as carving meat, preparing flambé dishes, or serving wine and liquor. Purchase or requisition supplies and equipment needed to ensure quality and timely delivery of services. Collaborate with other personnel to plan menus, serving arrangements, and related details. Supervise and check the assembly of regular and special diet trays and the delivery of food trolleys to hospital patients. Schedule parties and take reservations. Develop departmental objectives, budgets, policies, procedures, and strategies. Develop equipment maintenance schedules and arrange for repairs. Evaluate new products for usefulness and suitability.

Hottest Field Where They Work—Food Services and Drinking Places.

Work Conditions—Indoors; minor burns, cuts, bites, or stings; standing; walking and running; using hands on objects, tools, or controls; repetitive motions.

First-Line Supervisors/Managers of Office and Administrative Support Workers

- Level of Education/Training: Work experience in a related occupation
- Annual Earnings: $42,400
- Growth: 8.1%
- Annual Job Openings: 167,000
- Personality Type: Enterprising (ECS)

Applicants are likely to encounter keen competition because their numbers should greatly exceed the number of job openings.

On the Job—Supervise and coordinate the activities of clerical and administrative support workers. Resolve customer complaints and answer customers' questions regarding policies and procedures. Supervise the work of office, administrative, or customer service employees to ensure adherence to quality standards, deadlines, and proper procedures, correcting errors or problems. Provide employees with guidance in handling difficult or complex problems and in resolving escalated complaints or disputes. Implement corporate and departmental policies, procedures, and service standards in conjunction with management. Discuss job performance problems with employees in order to identify causes and issues and to work on resolving problems. Train and instruct employees in job duties and company policies or arrange for training to be provided. Evaluate employees' job performance and conformance to regulations and recommend appropriate personnel action. Recruit, interview, and select employees. Review records and reports pertaining to activities such as production, payroll, and shipping in order to verify details, monitor work activities, and evaluate performance. Interpret and communicate work procedures and company policies to staff. Prepare and issue work schedules, deadlines, and duty assignments of office or administrative staff. Maintain records pertaining to inventory, personnel, orders, supplies, and machine maintenance. Compute figures such as balances, totals, and commissions. Research, compile, and prepare reports, manuals, correspondence, and other information required by management or governmental agencies. Coordinate activities with other supervisory personnel and with other work units or departments. Analyze financial activities of establishments or departments and provide input into budget planning and preparation processes. Develop or update procedures, policies, and standards. Make recommendations to management concerning such issues as staffing decisions and procedural changes. Consult with managers and other personnel to resolve problems in areas such as equipment performance, output quality, and work schedules. Participate in the work of subordinates to facilitate productivity or to overcome difficult aspects of work.

Hottest Fields Where They Work—Health Care; Employment Services; Educational Services; Management, Scientific, and Technical Consulting Services; State and Local Government, Excluding Education and Hospitals.

Work Conditions—Indoors; noisy; sitting.

First-Line Supervisors/Managers of Retail Sales Workers

- Level of Education/Training: Work experience in a related occupation
- Annual Earnings: $32,840

- Growth: 3.8%
- Annual Job Openings: 229,000
- Personality Type: Enterprising (EC)

Long, irregular hours, including evenings and weekends, are common.

On the Job—Directly supervise sales workers in a retail establishment or department. Duties may include management functions, such as purchasing, budgeting, accounting, and personnel work, in addition to supervisory duties. Provide customer service by greeting and assisting customers and responding to customer inquiries and complaints. Assign employees to specific duties. Monitor sales activities to ensure that customers receive satisfactory service and quality goods. Direct and supervise employees engaged in sales, inventory-taking, reconciling cash receipts, or performing services for customers. Inventory stock and reorder when inventory drops to a specified level. Keep records of purchases, sales, and requisitions. Enforce safety, health, and security rules. Examine products purchased for resale or received for storage to assess the condition of each product or item. Hire, train, and evaluate personnel in sales or marketing establishments, promoting or firing workers when appropriate. Perform work activities of subordinates, such as cleaning and organizing shelves and displays and selling merchandise. Establish and implement policies, goals, objectives, and procedures for their department. Instruct staff on how to handle difficult and complicated sales. Formulate pricing policies for merchandise according to profitability requirements. Estimate consumer demand and determine the types and amounts of goods to be sold. Examine merchandise to ensure that it is correctly priced and displayed and that it functions as advertised. Plan and prepare work schedules and keep records of employees' work schedules and time cards. Review inventory and sales records to prepare reports for management and budget departments. Plan and coordinate advertising campaigns and sales promotions and prepare merchandise displays and advertising copy. Confer with company officials to develop methods and procedures to increase sales, expand markets, and promote business. Establish credit policies and operating procedures. Plan budgets and authorize payments and merchandise returns.

Hottest Fields Where They Work—Grocery Stores; Clothing, Accessory, and General Merchandise Stores; Automobile Dealers; Arts, Entertainment, and Recreation.

Work Conditions—Indoors; hazardous equipment; standing; walking and running; using hands on objects, tools, or controls.

Gaming Managers

- Level of Education/Training: Work experience in a related occupation
- Annual Earnings: $59,940
- Growth: 22.6%
- Annual Job Openings: 1,000
- Personality Type: Enterprising (EC)

Casino employees must pass a thorough background security check.

On the Job—Plan, organize, direct, control, or coordinate gaming operations in a casino. Formulate gaming policies for their area of responsibility. Resolve customer complaints regarding problems such as payout errors. Remove suspected cheaters, such as card counters and other players who may have systems that shift the odds of winning to their favor. Maintain familiarity with all games used at a facility, as well as strategies and tricks employed in those games. Train new workers and evaluate their performance. Circulate among gaming tables to ensure that operations are conducted properly, that dealers follow house rules, and that players are not cheating. Explain and interpret house rules, such as game rules and betting limits. Monitor staffing levels to ensure that games and tables are adequately staffed for each shift, arranging for staff rotations and breaks and locating substitute employees as necessary. Interview and hire workers. Prepare work schedules and station assignments and keep attendance records. Direct the distribution of complimentary hotel rooms, meals, and other discounts or free items given to players based on their length of play and betting totals. Establish policies on issues such as the type of gambling offered and the odds, the extension of credit, and the serving of food and beverages. Track supplies of money to tables and perform any required paperwork. Set and maintain a bank and table limit for each game. Monitor credit extended to players. Review operational expenses, budget estimates, betting accounts, and collection reports for accuracy. Record, collect, and pay off bets, issuing receipts as necessary. Direct workers compiling summary sheets that show wager amounts and payoffs for races and events. Notify board attendants of table vacancies so that waiting patrons can play.

Hottest Fields Where They Work—Arts, Entertainment, and Recreation; State and Local Government, Excluding Education and Hospitals; Hotels and Other Accommodations.

Work Conditions—Indoors; noisy; contaminants; standing; walking and running.

Enterprising Jobs Requiring Postsecondary Vocational Training

Appraisers, Real Estate

- Level of Education/Training: Postsecondary vocational training
- Annual Earnings: $43,440
- Growth: 22.8%
- Annual Job Openings: 9,000
- Personality Type: Enterprising (ECS)

The job openings listed here are shared with Assessors.

> Nearly 4 out of 10 are self-employed; salaried assessors worked primarily in local government, while salaried appraisers worked mainly for real estate firms.

On the Job—Appraise real property to determine its value for purchase, sales, investment, mortgage, or loan purposes. Prepare written reports that estimate property values, outline methods by which the estimations were made, and meet appraisal standards. Compute final estimation of property values, taking into account such factors as depreciation, replacement costs, value comparisons of similar properties, and income potential. Search public records for transactions such as sales, leases, and assessments. Inspect properties to evaluate construction, condition, special features, and functional design and to take property measurements. Photograph interiors and exteriors of properties to assist in estimating property value, substantiate findings, and complete appraisal reports. Evaluate land and neighborhoods where properties are situated, considering locations and trends or impending changes that could influence future values. Obtain county land values and sales information about nearby properties to aid in establishment of property values. Verify legal descriptions of properties by comparing them to county records. Check building codes and zoning bylaws to determine any effects on the properties being appraised. Estimate building replacement costs, using building valuation manuals and professional cost estimators. Examine income records and operating costs of income properties. Interview persons familiar with properties and immediate surroundings, such as contractors, homeowners, and real estate agents, to obtain pertinent information. Examine the type and location of nearby services such as shopping centers, schools, parks, and other neighborhood features to evaluate their impact on property values. Draw land diagrams that will be used in appraisal reports to support findings. Testify in court as to the value of a piece of real estate property.

Hottest Field Where They Work—State and Local Government, Excluding Education and Hospitals.

Work Conditions—More often outdoors than indoors; sitting.

Educational Program—Real Estate.

Enterprising Jobs Requiring an Associate Degree

Paralegals and Legal Assistants

- Level of Education/Training: Associate degree
- Annual Earnings: $41,170
- Growth: 29.7%
- Annual Job Openings: 28,000
- Personality Type: Enterprising (EC)

Competition for jobs should continue; experienced, formally trained paralegals should have the best employment opportunities.

On the Job—**Assist lawyers by researching legal precedent, investigating facts, or preparing legal documents. Conduct research to support a legal proceeding, to formulate a defense, or to initiate legal action.** Prepare legal documents, including briefs, pleadings, appeals, wills, contracts, and real estate closing statements. Prepare affidavits or other documents, maintain document file, and file pleadings with court clerk. Gather and analyze research data, such as statutes; decisions; and legal articles, codes, and documents. Investigate facts and law of cases to determine causes of action and to prepare cases. Call upon witnesses to testify at hearing. Direct and coordinate law office activity, including delivery of subpoenas. Arbitrate disputes between parties and assist in real estate closing process. Keep and monitor legal volumes to ensure that law library is up to date. Appraise and inventory real and personal property for estate planning.

Hottest Fields Where They Work—State and Local Government, Excluding Education and Hospitals; Employment Services; Insurance; Management, Scientific, and Technical Consulting Services; Federal Government, Excluding the Postal Service.

Work Conditions—Indoors; sitting; repetitive motions.

Educational Program—Legal Assistant/Paralegal.

Enterprising Jobs Requiring a Bachelor's Degree

Meeting and Convention Planners

- Level of Education/Training: Bachelor's degree
- Annual Earnings: $41,280
- Growth: 22.2%
- Annual Job Openings: 4,000
- Personality Type: Enterprising (ECS)

Opportunities will be best for individuals with a bachelor's degree and some meeting planning experience.

On the Job—Coordinate activities of staff and convention personnel to make arrangements for group meetings and conventions. Consult with customers to determine objectives and requirements for events such as meetings, conferences, and conventions. Monitor event activities to ensure compliance with applicable regulations and laws, satisfaction of participants, and resolution of any problems that arise. Confer with staff at a chosen event site to coordinate details. Plan and develop programs, agendas, budgets, and services according to customer requirements. Review event bills for accuracy and approve payment. Coordinate services for events, such as accommodation and transportation for participants, facilities, catering, signage, displays, special needs requirements, printing, and event security. Arrange for the availability of audiovisual equipment, transportation, displays, and other event needs. Inspect event facilities to ensure that they conform to customer requirements. Maintain records of event aspects, including financial details. Conduct post-event evaluations to determine how future events could be improved. Negotiate contracts with such service providers and suppliers as hotels, convention centers, and speakers. Meet with sponsors and organizing committees to plan scope and format of events, to establish and monitor budgets, or to review administrative procedures and event progress. Direct administrative details such as financial operations, dissemination of promotional materials, and responses to inquiries. Evaluate and select providers of services according to customer requirements. Read trade publications, attend seminars, and consult with other meeting professionals to keep abreast of meeting management standards and trends. Organize registration of event participants. Design and implement efforts to publicize events and promote sponsorships. Hire, train, and supervise volunteers and support staff required for events. Obtain permits from fire and health departments to erect displays and exhibits and serve food at events. Promote conference, convention, and trade show services by performing tasks such as meeting with professional and trade associations and producing brochures and other publications.

Hottest Fields Where They Work—Advocacy, Grantmaking, and Civic Organizations; Hotels and Other Accommodations; Educational Services; Management, Scientific, and Technical Consulting Services; Arts, Entertainment, and Recreation.

Work Conditions—Indoors; sitting.

Educational Program—Selling Skills and Sales Operations.

Personnel Recruiters

- Level of Education/Training: Bachelor's degree
- Annual Earnings: $41,780
- Growth: 30.5%
- Annual Job Openings: 30,000
- Personality Type: Enterprising (ES)

The job openings listed here are shared with Employment Interviewers.

The abundant supply of qualified college graduates and experienced workers should create keen competition for jobs.

On the Job—Seek out, interview, and screen applicants to fill existing and future job openings and promote career opportunities within an organization. Establish and maintain relationships with hiring managers to stay abreast of current and future hiring and business needs. Interview applicants to obtain information on work history, training, education, and job skills. Maintain current knowledge of Equal Employment Opportunity (EEO) and affirmative action guidelines and laws, such as the Americans with Disabilities Act (ADA). Perform searches for qualified candidates according to relevant job criteria, using computer databases, networking, Internet recruiting resources, cold calls, media, recruiting firms, and employee referrals. Prepare and maintain employment records. Contact applicants to inform them of employment possibilities, consideration, and selection. Inform potential applicants about facilities, operations, benefits, and job or career opportunities in organizations. Screen and refer applicants to hiring personnel in the organization, making hiring recommendations when appropriate. Arrange for interviews and provide travel arrangements as necessary. Advise managers and employees on staffing policies and procedures. Review and evaluate applicant qualifications or eligibility for specified licensing according to established guidelines and designated licensing codes. Hire applicants and authorize paperwork assigning them to positions. Conduct reference and background checks on applicants. Evaluate recruitment and selection criteria to ensure conformance to professional, statistical, and testing standards, recommending revision as needed.

145

Recruit applicants for open positions, arranging job fairs with college campus representatives. Advise management on organizing, preparing, and implementing recruiting and retention programs. Supervise personnel clerks performing filing, typing, and recordkeeping duties. Project yearly recruitment expenditures for budgetary consideration and control. Serve on selection and examination boards to evaluate applicants according to test scores, contacting promising candidates for interviews. Address civic and social groups and attend conferences to disseminate information concerning possible job openings and career opportunities.

Hottest Fields Where They Work—Employment Services; Management, Scientific, and Technical Consulting Services; Social Assistance, Except Child Day Care; State and Local Government, Excluding Education and Hospitals; Educational Services.

Work Conditions—Indoors; sitting.

Educational Programs—Human Resources Management/Personnel Administration, General; Labor and Industrial Relations.

Public Relations Specialists

- Level of Education/Training: Bachelor's degree
- Annual Earnings: $45,020
- Growth: 22.9%
- Annual Job Openings: 38,000
- Personality Type: Enterprising (EAS)

Although employment is projected to grow faster than average, keen competition is expected for entry-level jobs.

On the Job—Engage in promoting or creating good will for individuals, groups, or organizations by writing or selecting favorable publicity material and releasing it through various communications media. May prepare and arrange displays and make speeches. Prepare or edit organizational publications for internal and external audiences, including employee newsletters and stockholders' reports. Respond to requests for information from the media or designate another appropriate spokesperson or information source. Establish and maintain cooperative relationships with representatives of community, consumer, employee, and public interest groups. Plan and direct development and communication of informational programs to maintain favorable public and stockholder perceptions of an organization's accomplishments and agenda. Confer with production and support personnel to produce or coordinate production of advertisements and promotions. Arrange public appearances, lectures, contests, or exhibits for clients to increase product and service awareness and to promote goodwill. Study the objectives, promotional policies, and needs of organizations to develop public relations strategies that will influence public opinion or promote ideas, products, and services. Consult with advertising agencies or staff to arrange promotional campaigns in all types of media for products, organizations, or individuals. Confer with other managers to identify trends and key group interests and concerns or to provide advice on business decisions. Coach client representatives in effective communication with the public and with employees. Prepare and deliver speeches to further public relations objectives. Purchase advertising space and time as required to promote client's product or agenda. Plan and conduct market and public opinion research to test products or determine potential for product success, communicating results to client or management.

Hottest Fields Where They Work—Advertising and Public Relations Services; Advocacy, Grantmaking, and Civic Organizations; Educational Services; Health Care; Management, Scientific, and Technical Consulting Services.

Work Conditions—Indoors; sitting.

Educational Programs—Communication Studies/Speech Communication and Rhetoric; Public Relations/Image Management; Political Communication; Health Communication; Family and Consumer Sciences/Human Sciences Communication.

Conventional Jobs Requiring Short-Term On-the-Job Training

Bill and Account Collectors

- Level of Education/Training: Short-term on-the-job training
- Annual Earnings: $28,160
- Growth: 21.4%
- Annual Job Openings: 85,000
- Personality Type: Conventional (CE)

About 1 in 5 collectors works for a collection agency; others work in banks, retail stores, government, physicians' offices, hospitals, and other institutions that lend money and extend credit.

On the Job—Locate and notify customers of delinquent accounts by mail, telephone, or personal visit to solicit payment. Duties include receiving payment and posting amount to customer's account, preparing statements to credit department if customer fails to respond, initiating repossession proceedings or service disconnection, and keeping records of collection and status of accounts.

Receive payments and post amounts paid to customer accounts. Locate and monitor overdue accounts, using computers and a variety of automated systems. Record information about financial status of customers and status of collection efforts. Locate and notify customers of delinquent accounts by mail, telephone, or personal visits to solicit payment. Confer with customers by telephone or in person to determine reasons for overdue payments and to review the terms of sales, service, or credit contracts. Advise customers of necessary actions and strategies for debt repayment. Persuade customers to pay amounts due on credit accounts, damage claims, or nonpayable checks or to return merchandise. Sort and file correspondence and perform miscellaneous clerical duties such as answering correspondence and writing reports. Perform various administrative functions for assigned accounts, such as recording address changes and purging the records of deceased customers. Arrange for debt repayment or establish repayment schedules based on customers' financial situations. Negotiate credit extensions when necessary. Trace delinquent customers to new addresses by inquiring at post offices, telephone companies, or credit bureaus or through the questioning of neighbors. Notify credit departments, order merchandise repossession or service disconnection, and turn over account records to attorneys when customers fail to respond to collection attempts. Drive vehicles to visit customers, return merchandise to creditors, or deliver bills.

Hottest Fields Where They Work—Health Care; Employment Services; Wholesale Trade.

Work Conditions—Indoors; sitting; using hands on objects, tools, or controls; repetitive motions.

Interviewers, Except Eligibility and Loan

- Level of Education/Training: Short-term on-the-job training
- Annual Earnings: $25,110
- Growth: 26.0%
- Annual Job Openings: 43,000
- Personality Type: Conventional (CSE)

Because interviewers deal with the public, they must have a pleasant personality, clear speaking voice, and professional appearance. Familiarity with computers and strong interpersonal skills are very important.

On the Job—Interview persons by telephone, by mail, in person, or by other means for the purpose of completing forms, applications, or questionnaires. Ask specific questions, record answers, and assist persons with completing form.

May sort, classify, and file forms. Ask questions in accordance with instructions to obtain various specified information such as person's name, address, age, religious preference, and state of residency. Identify and resolve inconsistencies in interviewees' responses by means of appropriate questioning or explanation. Compile, record, and code results and data from interview or survey, using computer or specified form. Review data obtained from interview for completeness and accuracy. Contact individuals to be interviewed at home, place of business, or field location by telephone, by mail, or in person. Assist individuals in filling out applications or questionnaires. Ensure payment for services by verifying benefits with the person's insurance provider or working out financing options. Identify and report problems in obtaining valid data. Explain survey objectives and procedures to interviewees and interpret survey questions to help interviewees' comprehension. Perform patient services, such as answering the telephone and assisting patients with financial and medical questions. Prepare reports to provide answers in response to specific problems. Locate and list addresses and households. Perform other office duties as needed, such as telemarketing and customer service inquiries, billing patients, and receiving payments. Meet with supervisor daily to submit completed assignments and discuss progress. Collect and analyze data, such as studying old records; tallying the number of outpatients entering each day or week; or participating in federal, state, or local population surveys as a Census Enumerator.

Hottest Fields Where They Work—Health Care; Educational Services.

Work Conditions—Indoors; sitting; using hands on objects, tools, or controls; repetitive motions.

Office Clerks, General

- Level of Education/Training: Short-term on-the-job training
- Annual Earnings: $23,070
- Growth: 8.4%
- Annual Job Openings: 695,000
- Personality Type: Conventional (C)

Prospects should be best for those with knowledge of basic computer applications and office machinery as well as good communication skills.

On the Job—Perform duties too varied and diverse to be classified in any specific office clerical occupation requiring limited knowledge of office management systems and procedures. Clerical duties may be assigned in accordance with the office procedures of individual establishments and may include a combination of answering telephones, bookkeeping, typing or word processing, stenography,

office machine operation, and filing. Collect, count, and disburse money; do basic bookkeeping; and complete banking transactions. Communicate with customers, employees, and other individuals to answer questions, disseminate or explain information, take orders, and address complaints. Answer telephones, direct calls, and take messages. Compile, copy, sort, and file records of office activities, business transactions, and other activities. Complete and mail bills, contracts, policies, invoices, or checks. Operate office machines, such as photocopiers and scanners, facsimile machines, voice mail systems, and personal computers. Compute, record, and proofread data and other information, such as records or reports. Maintain and update filing, inventory, mailing, and database systems either manually or by using a computer. Open, sort, and route incoming mail; answer correspondence; and prepare outgoing mail. Review files, records, and other documents to obtain information to respond to requests. Deliver messages and run errands. Inventory and order materials, supplies, and services. Complete work schedules, manage calendars, and arrange appointments. Process and prepare documents, such as business or government forms and expense reports. Monitor and direct the work of lower-level clerks. Type, format, proofread, and edit correspondence and other documents from notes or dictating machines, using computers or typewriters. Count, weigh, measure, or organize materials. Train other staff members to perform work activities, such as using computer applications. Prepare meeting agendas, attend meetings, and record and transcribe minutes. Troubleshoot problems involving office equipment, such as computer hardware and software. Make travel arrangements for office personnel.

Hottest Fields Where They Work—Employment Services; Health Care; Educational Services; Management, Scientific, and Technical Consulting Services.

Work Conditions—Indoors; sitting; using hands on objects, tools, or controls.

Receptionists and Information Clerks

- Level of Education/Training: Short-term on-the-job training
- Annual Earnings: $22,150
- Growth: 21.7%
- Annual Job Openings: 299,000
- Personality Type: Conventional (CES)

Receptionists and information clerks generally receive on-the-job training. However, employers often look for applicants who already possess certain skills, such as prior computer experience or answering telephones.

On the Job—Answer inquiries and obtain information for general public, customers, visitors, and other interested parties. Provide information regarding

activities conducted at establishment and location of departments, offices, and employees within organization. Operate telephone switchboard to answer, screen, and forward calls, providing information, taking messages, and scheduling appointments. Receive payment and record receipts for services. Perform administrative support tasks such as proofreading; transcribing handwritten information; and operating calculators or computers to work with pay records, invoices, balance sheets, and other documents. Greet persons entering establishment, determine nature and purpose of visit, and direct or escort them to specific destinations. Hear and resolve complaints from customers and public. File and maintain records. Transmit information or documents to customers, using computer, mail, or facsimile machine. Schedule appointments and maintain and update appointment calendars. Analyze data to determine answers to questions from customers or members of the public. Provide information about establishment such as location of departments or offices, employees within the organization, or services provided. Keep a current record of staff members' whereabouts and availability. Collect, sort, distribute, and prepare mail, messages, and courier deliveries. Calculate and quote rates for tours, stocks, insurance policies, or other products and services. Take orders for merchandise or materials and send them to the proper departments to be filled. Process and prepare memos, correspondence, travel vouchers, or other documents. Schedule space and equipment for special programs and prepare lists of participants. Enroll individuals to participate in programs and notify them of their acceptance. Conduct tours or deliver talks describing features of public facility such as a historic site or national park. Perform duties such as taking care of plants and straightening magazines to maintain lobby or reception area.

Hottest Fields Where They Work—Health Care; Employment Services.

Work Conditions—Indoors; sitting; repetitive motions.

Shipping, Receiving, and Traffic Clerks

- Level of Education/Training: Short-term on-the-job training
- Annual Earnings: $25,180
- Growth: 3.7%
- Annual Job Openings: 121,000
- Personality Type: Conventional (CR)

Employers prefer to hire those familiar with computers and other electronic office and business equipment.

On the Job—Verify and keep records on incoming and outgoing shipments. Prepare items for shipment. Duties include assembling, addressing, stamping, and shipping merchandise or material; receiving, unpacking, verifying, and

recording incoming merchandise or material; and arranging for the transportation of products. Examine contents and compare with records such as manifests, invoices, or orders to verify accuracy of incoming or outgoing shipment. Prepare documents such as work orders, bills of lading, and shipping orders to route materials. Determine shipping method for materials, using knowledge of shipping procedures, routes, and rates. Record shipment data such as weight, charges, space availability, and damages and discrepancies for reporting, accounting, and record-keeping purposes. Contact carrier representative to make arrangements and to issue instructions for shipping and delivery of materials. Confer and correspond with establishment representatives to rectify problems such as damages, shortages, and nonconformance to specifications. Requisition and store shipping materials and supplies to maintain inventory of stock. Deliver or route materials to departments, using work devices, such as handtruck, conveyor, or sorting bins. Compute amounts such as space available and shipping, storage, and demurrage charges, using calculator or price list. Pack, seal, label, and affix postage to prepare materials for shipping, using work devices such as hand tools, power tools, and postage meter.

Hottest Fields Where They Work—Employment Services; Truck Transportation and Warehousing; Wholesale Trade; Clothing, Accessory, and General Merchandise Stores.

Work Conditions—Indoors; noisy; contaminants; sitting; walking and running; using hands on objects, tools, or controls.

Tellers

- Level of Education/Training: Short-term on-the-job training
- Annual Earnings: $21,300
- Growth: 6.8%
- Annual Job Openings: 108,000
- Personality Type: Conventional (CE)

Most job openings will arise from replacement needs because turnover is high.

On the Job—**Receive and pay out money. Keep records of money and negotiable instruments involved in a financial institution's various transactions.** Balance currency, coin, and checks in cash drawers at ends of shifts and calculate daily transactions, using computers, calculators, or adding machines. Cash checks and pay out money after verifying that signatures are correct, that written and numerical amounts agree, and that accounts have sufficient funds. Receive checks and cash for deposit, verify amounts, and check accuracy of deposit slips. Examine checks for endorsements and to verify other information such as dates, bank names, identification of the persons receiving payments, and the legality of the documents. Enter customers' transactions into computers to record transactions and issue computer-generated receipts. Count currency, coins, and checks received, by hand or using currency-counting machine, to prepare them for deposit or shipment to branch banks or the Federal Reserve Bank. Identify transaction mistakes when debits and credits do not balance. Prepare and verify cashier's checks. Arrange monies received in cash boxes and coin dispensers according to denomination. Process transactions such as term deposits, retirement savings plan contributions, automated teller transactions, night deposits, and mail deposits. Receive mortgage, loan, or public utility bill payments, verifying payment dates and amounts due. Resolve problems or discrepancies concerning customers' accounts. Explain, promote, or sell products or services such as travelers' checks, savings bonds, money orders, and cashier's checks, using computerized information about customers to tailor recommendations. Perform clerical tasks such as typing, filing, and microfilm photography. Monitor bank vaults to ensure cash balances are correct. Order a supply of cash to meet daily needs. Sort and file deposit slips and checks. Receive and count daily inventories of cash, drafts, and travelers' checks. Process and maintain records of customer loans. Count, verify, and post armored car deposits. Carry out special services for customers, such as ordering bank cards and checks. Compute financial fees, interest, and service charges. Obtain and process information required for the provision of services, such as opening accounts, savings plans, and purchasing bonds.

Hottest Field Where They Work—Banking.

Work Conditions—Indoors; more often standing than sitting; using hands on objects, tools, or controls; repetitive motions.

Conventional Jobs Requiring Moderate-Term On-the-Job Training

Bookkeeping, Accounting, and Auditing Clerks

- Level of Education/Training: Moderate-term on-the-job training
- Annual Earnings: $29,490
- Growth: 5.9%
- Annual Job Openings: 291,000
- Personality Type: Conventional (CE)

Those who can carry out a wider range of bookkeeping and accounting activities will be in greater demand than specialized clerks.

On the Job—Compute, classify, and record numerical data to keep financial records complete. Perform any combination of routine calculating, posting, and verifying duties to obtain primary financial data for use in maintaining accounting records. May also check the accuracy of figures, calculations, and postings pertaining to business transactions recorded by other workers. Operate computers programmed with accounting software to record, store, and analyze information. Check figures, postings, and documents for correct entry, mathematical accuracy, and proper codes. Comply with federal, state, and company policies, procedures, and regulations. Debit, credit, and total accounts on computer spreadsheets and databases, using specialized accounting software. Classify, record, and summarize numerical and financial data to compile and keep financial records, using journals and ledgers or computers. Calculate, prepare, and issue bills, invoices, account statements, and other financial statements according to established procedures. Code documents according to company procedures. Compile statistical, financial, accounting, or auditing reports and tables pertaining to such matters as cash receipts, expenditures, accounts payable and receivable, and profits and losses. Operate 10-key calculators, typewriters, and copy machines to perform calculations and produce documents. Access computerized financial information to answer general questions as well as those related to specific accounts. Reconcile or note and report discrepancies found in records. Perform financial calculations such as amounts due, interest charges, balances, discounts, equity, and principal. Perform general office duties such as filing, answering telephones, and handling routine correspondence. Prepare bank deposits by compiling data from cashiers; verifying and balancing receipts; and sending cash, checks, or other forms of payment to banks. Receive, record, and bank cash, checks, and vouchers. Calculate and prepare checks for utilities, taxes, and other payments. Compare computer printouts to manually maintained journals to determine if they match. Reconcile records of bank transactions. Prepare trial balances of books. Monitor status of loans and accounts to ensure that payments are up to date. Transfer details from separate journals to general ledgers or data processing sheets. Compile budget data and documents based on estimated revenues and expenses and previous budgets. Calculate costs of materials, overhead, and other expenses based on estimates, quotations, and price lists.

Hottest Fields Where They Work—Health Care; Employment Services; Management, Scientific, and Technical Consulting Services; Educational Services; Arts, Entertainment, and Recreation.

Work Conditions—Indoors; sitting; repetitive motions.

Customer Service Representatives

- Level of Education/Training: Moderate-term on-the-job training
- Annual Earnings: $27,490
- Growth: 22.8%
- Annual Job Openings: 510,000
- Personality Type: Conventional (CES)

Most jobs require only a high school diploma, but educational requirements are rising.

On the Job—Interact with customers to provide information in response to inquiries about products and services and to handle and resolve complaints. Confer with customers by telephone or in person to provide information about products and services, to take orders or cancel accounts, or to obtain details of complaints. Keep records of customer interactions and transactions, recording details of inquiries, complaints, and comments as well as actions taken. Resolve customers' service or billing complaints by performing activities such as exchanging merchandise, refunding money, and adjusting bills. Check to ensure that appropriate changes were made to resolve customers' problems. Contact customers to respond to inquiries or to notify them of claim investigation results and any planned adjustments. Refer unresolved customer grievances to designated departments for further investigation. Determine charges for services requested, collect deposits or payments, or arrange for billing. Complete contract forms, prepare change-of-address records, and issue service discontinuance orders, using computers. Obtain and examine all relevant information to assess validity of complaints and to determine possible causes, such as extreme weather conditions, that could increase utility bills. Solicit sale of new or additional services or products. Review insurance policy terms to determine whether a particular loss is covered by insurance. Review claims adjustments with dealers, examining parts claimed to be defective and approving or disapproving dealers' claims. Compare disputed merchandise with original requisitions and information from invoices and prepare invoices for returned goods. Order tests that could determine the causes of product malfunctions. Recommend improvements in products, packaging, shipping, service, or billing methods and procedures to prevent future problems.

Hottest Fields Where They Work—Employment Services; Insurance; Wholesale Trade; Health Care; Management, Scientific, and Technical Consulting Services.

Work Conditions—Indoors; sitting; using hands on objects, tools, or controls; repetitive motions.

Executive Secretaries and Administrative Assistants

- Level of Education/Training: Moderate-term on-the-job training
- Annual Earnings: $35,960
- Growth: 12.4%
- Annual Job Openings: 218,000
- Personality Type: Conventional (CE)

Opportunities should be best for applicants with extensive knowledge of software applications.

On the Job—Provide high-level administrative support by conducting research; preparing statistical reports; handling information requests; and performing clerical functions such as preparing correspondence, receiving visitors, arranging conference calls, and scheduling meetings. May also train and supervise lower-level clerical staff. Manage and maintain executives' schedules. Prepare invoices, reports, memos, letters, financial statements, and other documents, using word-processing, spreadsheet, database, or presentation software. Open, sort, and distribute incoming correspondence, including faxes and e-mail. Read and analyze incoming memos, submissions, and reports to determine their significance and plan their distribution. File and retrieve corporate documents, records, and reports. Greet visitors and determine whether they should be given access to specific individuals. Prepare responses to correspondence containing routine inquiries. Perform general office duties such as ordering supplies, maintaining records management systems, and performing basic bookkeeping work. Prepare agendas and make arrangements for committee, board, and other meetings. Make travel arrangements for executives. Conduct research, compile data, and prepare papers for consideration and presentation by executives, committees, and boards of directors. Compile, transcribe, and distribute minutes of meetings. Attend meetings to record minutes. Coordinate and direct office services, such as records and budget preparation, personnel, and housekeeping, to aid executives. Meet with individuals, special interest groups, and others on behalf of executives, committees, and boards of directors. Set up and oversee administrative policies and procedures for offices or organizations. Supervise and train other clerical staff. Review operating practices and procedures to determine whether improvements can be made in areas such as workflow, reporting procedures, or expenditures. Interpret administrative and operating policies and procedures for employees.

Hottest Fields Where They Work—Employment Services; Educational Services; Health Care; Management, Scientific, and Technical Consulting Services; State and Local Government, Excluding Education and Hospitals.

Work Conditions—Indoors; sitting; repetitive motions.

Pharmacy Technicians

- Level of Education/Training: Moderate-term on-the-job training
- Annual Earnings: $24,390
- Growth: 28.6%
- Annual Job Openings: 35,000
- Personality Type: Conventional (CR)

Many technicians work evenings, weekends, and holidays.

On the Job—**Prepare medications under the direction of a pharmacist. May measure, mix, count out, label, and record amounts and dosages of medications.** Receive written prescription or refill requests and verify that information is complete and accurate. Maintain proper storage and security conditions for drugs. Answer telephones, responding to questions or requests. Fill bottles with prescribed medications and type and affix labels. Assist customers by answering simple questions, locating items, or referring them to the pharmacist for medication information. Price and file prescriptions that have been filled. Clean and help maintain equipment and work areas and sterilize glassware according to prescribed methods. Establish and maintain patient profiles, including lists of medications taken by individual patients. Order, label, and count stock of medications, chemicals, and supplies and enter inventory data into computer. Receive and store incoming supplies, verify quantities against invoices, and inform supervisors of stock needs and shortages. Transfer medication from vials to the appropriate number of sterile, disposable syringes, using aseptic techniques. Add measured drugs or nutrients to intravenous solutions under sterile conditions to prepare intravenous (IV) packs under pharmacist supervision. Supply and monitor robotic machines that dispense medicine into containers and label the containers. Prepare and process medical insurance claim forms and records. Mix pharmaceutical preparations according to written prescriptions. Operate cash registers to accept payment from customers. Compute charges for medication and equipment dispensed to hospital patients and enter data in computer. Deliver medications and pharmaceutical supplies to patients, nursing stations, or surgery. Price stock and mark items for sale. Maintain and merchandise home health care products and services.

Hottest Fields Where They Work—Health Care; Clothing, Accessory, and General Merchandise Stores; Grocery Stores; Wholesale Trade.

157

Work Conditions—Indoors; standing; using hands on objects, tools, or controls; repetitive motions.

Conventional Jobs Requiring Work Experience in a Related Occupation

Construction and Building Inspectors

- Level of Education/Training: Work experience in a related occupation
- Annual Earnings: $44,720
- Growth: 22.3%
- Annual Job Openings: 6,000
- Personality Type: Conventional (CRI)

Opportunities should be best for experienced construction supervisors and craftworkers who have some college education, engineering or architectural training, or certification as construction inspectors or plan examiners.

On the Job—Inspect structures, using engineering skills, to determine structural soundness and compliance with specifications, building codes, and other regulations. Inspections may be general in nature or may be limited to a specific area, such as electrical systems or plumbing. Use survey instruments; metering devices; tape measures; and test equipment, such as concrete strength measurers, to perform inspections. Inspect bridges, dams, highways, buildings, wiring, plumbing, electrical circuits, sewers, heating systems, and foundations during and after construction for structural quality, general safety, and conformance to specifications and codes. Maintain daily logs and supplement inspection records with photographs. Review and interpret plans, blueprints, site layouts, specifications, and construction methods to ensure compliance to legal requirements and safety regulations. Inspect and monitor construction sites to ensure adherence to safety standards, building codes, and specifications. Measure dimensions and verify level, alignment, and elevation of structures and fixtures to ensure compliance to building plans and codes. Issue violation notices and stop-work orders, conferring with owners, violators, and authorities to explain regulations and recommend rectifications. Issue permits for construction, relocation, demolition, and occupancy. Approve and sign plans that meet required specifications. Compute estimates of work completed or of needed renovations or upgrades and approve payment for contractors. Monitor installation of plumbing, wiring, equipment, and appliances to ensure that installation is performed properly and is in compliance with applicable regulations. Examine lifting and conveying devices such as elevators, escalators, moving sidewalks, lifts and hoists, inclined railways, ski lifts, and amusement rides to ensure safety and proper functioning. Train, direct, and supervise other construction inspectors. Evaluate premises for cleanliness, including proper garbage disposal and lack of vermin infestation.

Hottest Field Where They Work—State and Local Government, Excluding Education and Hospitals.

Work Conditions—More often outdoors than indoors; noisy; contaminants; hazardous equipment; standing.

Conventional Jobs Requiring Postsecondary Vocational Training

Assessors

- Level of Education/Training: Postsecondary vocational training
- Annual Earnings: $43,440
- Growth: 22.8%
- Annual Job Openings: 9,000
- Personality Type: Conventional (CE)

The job openings listed here are shared with Appraisers, Real Estate.

Appraisers and assessors must meet licensing or certification requirements, which vary by state but generally include specific training requirements, a period of work as a trainee, and passing one or more examinations.

On the Job—**Appraise real and personal property to determine its fair value. May assess taxes in accordance with prescribed schedules.** Determine taxability and value of properties, using methods such as field inspection, structural measurement, calculation, sales analysis, market trend studies, and income and expense analysis. Inspect new construction and major improvements to existing structures to determine values. Explain assessed values to property owners and defend appealed assessments at public hearings. Inspect properties, considering factors such as market value, location, and building or replacement costs to determine appraisal value. Prepare and maintain current data on each parcel assessed, including maps of boundaries, inventories of land and structures, property characteristics, and any applicable exemptions. Identify the ownership of each piece of taxable property. Conduct regular reviews of property within jurisdictions to determine changes in property due to construction or demolition. Complete and maintain assessment rolls that show the assessed values and status of all property in a municipality. Issue notices of assessments and taxes. Review information about transfers of property to ensure its accuracy, checking basic information on buyers, sellers, and sales prices and making corrections as necessary. Maintain familiarity with aspects of local real estate markets. Analyze trends in sales prices, construction costs, and rents to assess property values or determine the accuracy of assessments. Approve applications for property tax exemptions or deductions. Establish uniform and equitable systems for assessing all classes and kinds of property. Write and submit appraisal and tax reports for public record. Serve on assessment review boards. Hire staff members. Provide sales analyses to be used for equalization of school aid. Calculate tax bills for properties by multiplying assessed values by jurisdiction tax rates.

Hottest Field Where They Work—State and Local Government, Excluding Education and Hospitals.

Work Conditions—More often indoors than outdoors; sitting; using hands on objects, tools, or controls; repetitive motions.

Educational Program—Real Estate.

Conventional Jobs Requiring an Associate Degree

Medical Records and Health Information Technicians

- Level of Education/Training: Associate degree
- Annual Earnings: $26,690
- Growth: 28.9%
- Annual Job Openings: 14,000
- Personality Type: Conventional (C)

This is one of the few health occupations in which there is little or no direct contact with patients.

On the Job—Compile, process, and maintain medical records of hospital and clinic patients in a manner consistent with medical, administrative, ethical, legal, and regulatory requirements of the health-care system. Process, maintain, compile, and report patient information for health requirements and standards. Protect the security of medical records to ensure that confidentiality is maintained. Process patient admission and discharge documents. Review records for completeness, accuracy, and compliance with regulations. Compile and maintain patients' medical records to document condition and treatment and to provide data for research or cost control and care improvement efforts. Enter data, such as demographic characteristics, history and extent of disease, diagnostic procedures, and treatment into computer. Release information to persons and agencies according to regulations. Plan, develop, maintain, and operate a variety of health record indexes and storage and retrieval systems to collect, classify, store, and analyze information. Manage the department and supervise clerical workers, directing and controlling activities of personnel in the medical records department. Transcribe medical reports. Identify, compile, abstract, and code patient data, using standard classification systems. Resolve or clarify codes and diagnoses with conflicting, missing, or unclear information by consulting with doctors or others or by participating in the coding team's regular meetings. Train medical records staff. Assign the patient to diagnosis-related groups (DRGs), using appropriate computer software. Post medical insurance billings. Process and prepare business and government forms. Contact discharged patients, their families, and physicians to maintain registry with follow-up information, such as quality of life and length of survival of cancer patients. Prepare statistical reports, narrative reports, and graphic presentations of information such as tumor registry data for use by hospital staff, researchers, or other users. Consult classification manuals to locate information about disease processes. Compile medical care and census data for statistical reports on diseases treated, surgery performed, or use of hospital beds. Develop in-service educational materials.

Hottest Field Where They Work—Health Care.

Work Conditions—Indoors; noisy; sitting; using hands on objects, tools, or controls; repetitive motions.

Educational Programs—Health Information/Medical Records Technology/ Technician; Medical Insurance Coding Specialist/Coder.

Conventional Jobs Requiring a Bachelor's Degree

Accountants

- Level of Education/Training: Bachelor's degree
- Annual Earnings: $52,210
- Growth: 22.4%
- Annual Job Openings: 157,000
- Personality Type: Conventional (CE)

The job openings listed here are shared with Auditors.

Overall job opportunities should be favorable; job seekers who obtain professional recognition through certification or licensure, a master's degree, proficiency in accounting and auditing computer software, or specialized expertise will have the best opportunities.

On the Job—Analyze financial information and prepare financial reports to determine or maintain record of assets, liabilities, profit and loss, tax liability, or other financial activities within an organization. Prepare, examine, or analyze accounting records, financial statements, or other financial reports to assess accuracy, completeness, and conformance to reporting and procedural standards. Compute taxes owed and prepare tax returns, ensuring compliance with payment, reporting, or other tax requirements. Analyze business operations, trends, costs, revenues, financial commitments, and obligations to project future revenues and expenses or to provide advice. Report to management regarding the finances of establishment. Establish tables of accounts and assign entries to proper accounts. Develop, maintain, and analyze budgets, preparing periodic reports that compare budgeted costs to actual costs. Develop, implement, modify, and document recordkeeping and accounting systems, making use of current computer technology. Prepare forms and manuals for accounting and bookkeeping personnel and direct their work activities. Survey operations to ascertain accounting needs and to recommend, develop, or maintain solutions to business and financial problems. Work as Internal Revenue Service (IRS) agents. Advise management about issues such as resource utilization, tax strategies, and the assumptions underlying budget forecasts. Provide internal and external auditing services for businesses or individuals. Advise clients in areas such as compensation, employee health care benefits, the design of accounting or data processing systems, or long-range tax or estate plans. Investigate bankruptcies and other complex financial transactions and prepare reports summarizing the findings. Represent clients before taxing authorities and provide support during litigation involving financial issues. Appraise, evaluate, and inventory real property and equipment, recording information such as the description, value, and location of property. Maintain or examine the records of government agencies. Serve as bankruptcy trustees or business valuators.

Hottest Fields Where They Work—Educational Services; Health Care; Management, Scientific, and Technical Consulting Services; Employment Services; Wholesale Trade.

Work Conditions—Indoors; sitting.

Educational Programs—Accounting and Computer Science; Accounting; Accounting and Finance; Accounting and Business/Management.

Auditors

- Level of Education/Training: Bachelor's degree
- Annual Earnings: $52,210
- Growth: 22.4%
- Annual Job Openings: 157,000
- Personality Type: Conventional (CE)

The job openings listed here are shared with Accountants.

An increase in the number of businesses, changing financial laws and regulations, and greater scrutiny of company finances will drive faster-than-average growth of accountants and auditors.

On the Job—Examine and analyze accounting records to determine financial status of establishment and prepare financial reports concerning operating procedures. Collect and analyze data to detect deficient controls; duplicated effort; extravagance; fraud; or non-compliance with laws, regulations, and management policies. Report to management about asset utilization and audit results and recommend changes in operations and financial activities. Prepare detailed reports on audit findings. Review data about material assets, net worth, liabilities, capital stock, surplus, income, and expenditures. Inspect account books and accounting systems for efficiency, effectiveness, and use of accepted accounting procedures to record transactions. Examine and evaluate financial and information systems, recommending controls to ensure system reliability and data integrity. Supervise auditing of establishments and determine scope of investigation required. Prepare, analyze, and verify annual reports, financial statements, and other records, using accepted accounting and statistical procedures to assess financial condition and facilitate financial planning. Confer with company officials about financial and regulatory matters. Inspect cash on hand, notes receivable and payable, negotiable securities, and canceled checks to confirm records are accurate. Examine inventory to verify journal and ledger entries. Examine whether the organization's objectives are reflected in its management activities and whether employees understand the objectives. Examine records and interview workers to ensure recording of transactions and compliance with laws and regulations. Direct activities of personnel engaged in filing, recording, compiling, and transmitting financial records. Produce up-to-the-minute information, using internal computer systems, to allow management to base decisions on actual, not historical, data. Conduct pre-implementation audits to determine if systems and programs under development will work as planned. Review taxpayer accounts and conduct audits on-site, by correspondence, or by summoning taxpayer to office. Evaluate taxpayer finances to determine tax liability, using knowledge of interest and discount rates, annuities, valuation of stocks and bonds, and amortization valuation of depletable assets.

Hottest Fields Where They Work—Educational Services; Health Care; Management, Scientific, and Technical Consulting Services; Employment Services; Wholesale Trade.

Work Conditions—Indoors; noisy; sitting; using hands on objects, tools, or controls; repetitive motions.

Educational Programs—Accounting and Computer Science; Accounting; Auditing; Accounting and Finance; Accounting and Business/Management.

Key Points: Chapter 5

- Personality is not the only thing to consider when you think about jobs. Many other factors will contribute to your satisfaction.
- The job snapshots can help you narrow down your choices. Be sure to investigate further before you make your final choice of a career goal, and keep another job in mind as Plan B.

Chapter 6

What If I Don't Have the Right Training and Education for a Hot Career?

E ducation and training are the keys to career advancement. This chapter focuses on how to build your skills and credentials so you'll be a hot job candidate.

It's true that for one-third of the jobs in this book, no previous postsecondary education or training is normally required because employers train new hires at the workplace in how to do the job. But it's also true that you'll be more impressive at the job interview if you have evidence of some related skills. For example, Executive Secretaries and Administrative Assistants learn their jobs through on-the-job training that lasts anywhere from one month to a year. But employers for this job are unlikely to hire job candidates who have never used word-processing software. And applicants who already know how to use spreadsheets or scheduling software are particularly qualified.

It's also possible that you are considering one or more hot jobs that do have formal requirements for education or training. You may be wondering how to acquire these credentials.

Finally, you may be looking down the road at what you will need to do *after* you are hired to advance in your career. Even staying in the same job will require continuous learning. Technology is constantly advancing, businesses are reaching out to new markets, and you'll need new skills to keep pace with these changes.

Fortunately, businesses and educational institutions are aware of the need for lifelong learning, so opportunities for acquiring new skills are better now than they have ever been—if you are willing to take the initiative to seek them out.

Informal Learning

If you're already working, even part-time, you can develop your skills on the job and thus prepare for one of the hot jobs. When you see co-workers using skills that you don't have, watch what they do and ask them to show you how. When you feel you have mastered the skill, ask your supervisor for an assignment that uses the skill—perhaps not a high-stakes project, but something that will demonstrate your new skill. Then be sure to ask for feedback that specifically targets your use of the skill. What did you do right? How could you have done it better? Try not to be defensive in response to criticism; use this feedback as part of the learning process.

If you're not working now, you can get informal on-the-job training in specific skills by doing volunteer work in a relevant setting. For example, to improve your people skills, do volunteer work at a senior center, a charity fund-raising event, or some other setting where there's a lot of interaction with people. Some hobbies also provide opportunities for you to learn skills—for example, designing Web pages, customizing cars, or gardening. With hobbies it helps to join a club so you can learn from more highly skilled hobbyists and get feedback on your accomplishments. Just keep in mind that your volunteer work can do more than just help others and your hobby can be more than just a self-indulgence. Use them as skill academies. Challenge yourself with new tasks; ask for feedback.

Sometimes you can create your own training program by studying a book or technical manual (maybe one aimed at "dummies"). In fact, if the skill you want to learn is very rare (for example, speaking Estonian) or on the cutting edge of technology (for example, using the very latest software programs), you may have no choice but to design your own curriculum because you can't find anyone to teach you. If you're very lucky, you may be able to convince your employer to pay for the books or other learning aids and to give you time in the workday for upgrading your skills. But most workers find that they have to use lunch hours, evenings, and weekends for this self-training. Consider the time and expense of self-training as investments in your future employability.

> **Tip:** *Try to find a study partner to learn with you; study partners help reinforce each other's learning and keep the learning program on track.*

College Credit for What You Already Know

If you have learned a lot informally, you may be able to get college credit for your accomplishments. Having a transcript with college credit can give a boost to your career and can take you at least partway toward completing a degree. Keep in mind that all of the methods described here involve fees, but they are cheaper than paying tuition and may fit into your schedule better than taking classes.

Several "colleges without walls" specialize in granting credit for experiential learning; you can get credit, even a degree, without visiting the college or residing in its state. But to prove you have learned at the college level, you need to assemble a portfolio of your work, something a lot more detailed than a statement on a resume.

Colleges Offering Credit for Portfolios

Thomas Edison State College: www.tesc.edu

Charter Oak State College: www.charteroak.edu

Excelsior College: www.excelsior.edu

Another way to prove your learning and get college credit is by taking a test. The College-Level Examination Program (CLEP) is the best-known program of this kind, and its credits are more widely accepted than those from any other such program. The tests are multiple choice and take 90 minutes. You can probably find study guides for specific CLEP tests at your local library. Other programs of this kind are DSST, which started in the military as the DANTES program; the Excelsior College Examinations; and the Thomas Edison College Examination Program (TECEP).

Credit by Examination

CLEP: www.collegeboard.com/clep

DSST: www.getcollegecredit.com

Excelsior College Examinations: www.excelsior.edu

TECEP: www.tesc.edu/students/tecep/tecep.php

College Credit for Military Training

If you have acquired college-level skills in military training, you may want to use one of the examination programs discussed in the previous section. But you may be able to obtain college credit more directly. Many colleges follow the recommendations of the American Council on Education in awarding college credit for specific military experiences. The ACE guide is online at www.militaryguides.acenet.edu.

> **Tip:** *Some employers use the ACE guide to recognize military experiences that are equivalent to academic coursework. You may be able to convince an employer that your military service gives you the credentials needed for the job.*

Beware of Scams

Because there is such a demand for education and the costs of education have risen rapidly, a lot of companies are offering bogus degrees. Some of these "universities" have impressive-sounding names, often similar to the names of prestigious colleges. They may advertise on the border of your computer screen when you're looking at a completely legitimate Web site. Or you may get an e-mail urging you to gain academic credit for life experience, just as you can from the genuine programs listed in this chapter. For example, they may offer to grant you a bachelor's degree for $500. These are really diploma mills that exist only to give phony credentials.

As in all cases of fraud, if it sounds too good to be true, it probably is. And you should never consider using a phony degree to pad your resume. It's against the law in a growing number of states, and law enforcement officials are investigating diploma mills and publicizing their names so employers will be on the lookout.

Formal Learning

Some skills can be learned only in formal settings. Secondary School Teachers, for example, need a college degree and often need specific courses in education. In the previous section you saw some ways to get college credit for informal learning. Now let's look at some legitimate shortcuts that can help you speed up the process of getting educational credentials through formal classes.

Entering Without Full Credentials

Very few of the jobs in this book have educational requirements that are spelled out by law. And because these are fast-growing jobs, in some cases you can find employers who will be willing to hire highly skilled and motivated job candidates who do not have the formal credentials that normally are expected. For example, in some communities and for some subjects, teachers are being hired even though their college degree is not in education. These "alternate entry route" teachers need to have expertise in their subject, they need to be good at communicating and comfortable with young people, and they need to be willing to start taking evening and summer classes in education—but the school district is willing to waive normal requirements because vacancies need to be filled.

You may be able to make a similar arrangement with an employer who is open-minded or simply hungry for workers. Note that you must have skills that make up for your lack of formal credentials, and it may be necessary for you to work toward obtaining that expected piece of paper. It can help for you to have some kind of partial credential—for example, an associate degree when a bachelor's might normally be expected or a smattering of courses in a relevant subject when an associate degree is the norm. The employer may think of this as a down payment on your future education—and, if you're lucky, your employer may even help pay for you to complete your degree.

Single Classes and Workshops

Sometimes a degree is not as important as single classes in highly job-relevant subjects—particularly for advancing in your job when you already have a degree. Night schools and corporate training centers offer classes in technical skills, such as using spreadsheets or driving trucks, or in "soft" skills, such as conducting meetings or reading people's body language. Another setting for training is the annual conference of the professional association relevant to your career, where you can attend training workshops.

Because the need for these popular skills is so obvious, employers often are willing to cover the expenses and perhaps the time these classes require. Be sure to find out what classes your employer makes available and consider taking them if they are at all relevant to your work. Your employer will appreciate your desire to upgrade your skills.

Sometimes employers are not willing to set aside funding or time for classes that would add to your skills, especially if your workday is very busy or if the skills you are seeking are not obviously relevant to your job. In fact, your employer may fear that you would use your new skills to find work elsewhere—and, in fact, that is another good reason for upgrading your skills. If your employer is unwilling to help or you are not currently employed, you may need to find (and pay for) useful night classes at your local high school, vocational school, or community college. Alternatively, it may be worthwhile for you to invest your time and money in a very relevant night class at a proprietary technical school (or "institute"), but first be sure to get evidence that employers will value this credential.

Key Points: Chapter 6

- Education and training make you a better job candidate and improve your chances of advancing in your career.

- A lot of learning can take place in informal settings, free of charge, but you need to take the initiative to make it happen.

- You can complete many of the requirements for a college degree without setting foot in a classroom or paying expensive tuition bills, but you need to be sure to use legitimate, widely accepted programs.

Chapter 7

Quick Tips for Getting a Hot Job

Previous chapters have helped you to target the hot careers that match your interests and to consider the education and training you will need for them. You have set your sights on the goal, and now it is time to reach for that goal: to get hired in the hot job that is out there waiting for you. This chapter illustrates quick but helpful techniques you can use to shorten the time it takes to get a job.

Finding and Targeting Hot Jobs

The good news is that the kinds of jobs listed in this book should not be as hard to find as most, especially in the metropolitan areas where these jobs are growing fastest. After all, if these jobs weren't plentiful or growing, they wouldn't be in this book and you probably wouldn't be interested in them.

The bad news is that many other people will be interested in them as well. So while there may be lots of opportunities available, there may also be intense competition, and openings will fill quickly. Using the job search strategies found in this chapter can give you an advantage over other job seekers, helping you to get the job you want before most others even know it is available.

Two Very Important Points About Job Search Methods

We want to make two points that apply to all job search methods:

1. **It is unwise to rely on just one or two job search methods.** You should use every option available to you, including networking and responding to job postings online and off. Industries and businesses experiencing growth will often need to find new workers quickly and will use a variety of methods to locate prospective candidates. The more methods you use, the better chance you have of finding those employers—and of their finding you.

(continued)

(continued)

2. **It is essential that you take an active rather than a passive approach in your job search.** You can't sit back and wait for employers to call you. You must talk to people, use the available resources, and find the jobs yourself. After all, these are hot careers, with job opportunities that are filled almost as soon as they are opened or advertised.

Traditional Job Search Methods

It is true that jobs that are in demand are more likely to be advertised. Open the classifieds or visit an online job posting site and you will probably see openings for many if not most of the fastest-growing jobs in this book. That is one advantage of hot jobs: Their demand often makes them easier to find.

Even knowing this, however, *only* replying to classified and Internet ads drastically reduces your chances of finding and getting the job you want. A recent *New York Times* survey showed that fewer than 15 percent of all job seekers get jobs from responding to want ads and online job postings. In fact, traditional job search methods tend to be ineffective as a whole. Here is more detail on the effectiveness of seven of the most popular traditional job search methods:

> **Tip:** On average, job seekers spend fewer than 15 hours a week looking for work. The average length of unemployment varies, but many job seekers are out of work three or more months, some far longer. There is a clear connection between how long it takes to find a job and the number of hours spent looking on a daily and weekly basis: The more time you spend on your job search each week, the less time you are likely to remain unemployed.

- **Help-wanted ads and online postings:** Everyone who reads the paper or visits the job sites knows about these openings, so competition for advertised jobs is fierce. Still, some people get jobs through ads, so go ahead and apply. Just be sure to spend most of your time using more effective methods.

- **State employment services:** Each state has a network of local offices to provide job leads and other services free of charge. Nationally, only about 5 percent of all job seekers get their jobs here, and these offices typically know of only one-tenth (or fewer) of the job openings in a region.

- **Private employment agencies:** These agencies work best for entry-level positions or for people with specialized, in-demand skills. The success record of these businesses is quite modest, however, and such agencies charge a fee as high as 20 percent of your annual salary to you or to the employer. Also keep in mind that most private agencies find job openings by calling employers, something you could do yourself.

- **Sending out resumes:** One survey found that you would have to mail more than 500 unsolicited resumes to get one interview. Like other traditional approaches, use this method sparingly because the numbers are stacked against you. A better approach is to contact the person who might hire you, by phone or via e-mail, to set up an interview directly—and then send a cover letter and resume.

- **Filling out applications:** Most applications are used to screen you out. Larger organizations may require them, but remember that your task is to get an interview, not fill out an application. If you do complete applications, make them neat and error-free and do not include anything that could get you screened out.

> **Tip:** *If necessary, leave a problem question or section blank on an application. You can always explain it after you get an interview.*

- **Human resource departments:** Hardly anyone gets hired by interviewers in HR or personnel departments. Their job is to screen you and then refer the "best" applicants to the person who would supervise you. You may need to cooperate with the people in HR, but it is often better to go directly to the person who has the authority to make you a job offer.

No matter where you hunt for jobs, you may have trouble finding job openings if you look for them using the wrong occupational title. For example, you may search the classified ads for Respiratory Therapist, not knowing that job openings are advertised under Inhalation Therapist, Oxygen Therapist, or Respiratory Care Practitioner. Before you start your job hunt, research your target occupation in greater detail and find out what alternate job titles are sometimes used. The appendix suggests sources for further career exploration.

The Two Job Search Methods That Work Best: Warm and Cold Contacts

One survey found that about 85 percent of all employers don't advertise their job openings. They hire people they know, people who find out about the jobs through word of mouth, or people who happen to be in the right place at the right time. In fact, about two-thirds of all people get their jobs using informal methods. These jobs are often not advertised and are part of the "hidden" job market.

The key to quickly getting any job, hot or not, is to find it and go after it before it is even posted. How? There are two basic informal job search methods: networking with people you know (which we call warm contacts) and making direct contact with an employer (which we call cold contacts). They are both based on the most important job search rule of all:

The Most Important Job Search Rule:

Don't wait until the job is open before contacting the employer!

The trick is to meet people who can hire you *before* a job is available. And because the jobs in this book are growing fast or have a large number of openings, odds are one will become available before you know it.

Warm Contacts—How to Start Developing Your Network

One study found that about 40 percent of all people found their jobs through a lead provided by a friend, a relative, or an acquaintance. Not only do these warm contacts provide actual job leads, they also provide access to additional contacts. Developing new contacts is called "networking," and here's how it works:

1. **Make lists of people you know.** Develop a list of anyone with whom you are friendly; then make a separate list of all your relatives. Next, think of other groups with whom you have something in common, such as former co-workers or classmates, members of your social or sports groups, members of your professional association, former employers, and members of your religious group. You may not know many of these people personally, but most will help you if you ask them.

2. **Contact the people on your lists in a systematic way.** Each of these people is a contact for you. Obviously, some people will be more helpful than others, but almost any one of them could help you find a job lead.

3. **Present yourself well.** Begin with your friends and relatives. Call or e-mail them and tell them you are looking for a job and need their help. Be as clear as possible about what you are looking for and what skills and qualifications you have.

4. **Ask them for leads.** It is possible that they will know of a job opening that is just right for you. If so, get the details and get right on it! More likely, however, they will not, so ask them for the name of someone who might.

5. **Contact these referrals and ask them the same questions.** For each original contact, you can extend your network of acquaintances by hundreds of people. Eventually, one of these people will hire you or refer you to someone who will.

If you know the industry or field you would like to work in, you can increase your networking potential by going to events attended by people with similar interests or sponsored by associations from that industry. Professional association meetings, conferences, lectures, and classes all provide an opportunity to network with people in that field.

Networking is about much more than asking people if they know of any job openings. The answer is likely to be no. Instead, look at networking as a way to build relationships with people who know other people who may know of jobs. Networking is also about getting advice about your search and insight into the organizations you're trying to break into.

You may also look on networking as the last stage of career exploration: It can help you learn about the job market for your career goal. That knowledge may shape your thinking about your career plans—for example, it may lead you to pursue the job in one field or specialization rather than another.

The appendix lists a valuable resource with detailed suggestions for improving your networking efforts.

Cold Contacts—Using the Telephone to Get Interviews

Once you get used to it, making direct contacts by phone is easy and effective. Most employers don't mind talking to a person they might be interested in hiring. Because most phone calls take only a minute or two, you can easily make personal contact with more than 20 employers in one morning.

Online sites like www.yellowpages.com and others allow you to find potential employers anywhere, but the print version is best if you're looking for a local job. Use the index to find businesses in the industries or fields that interest you. Then call the businesses and ask to speak to the person who is most likely to hire or supervise you.

> **Tip:** Instead of calling, you could try just walking into a business or organization that interests you and asking to speak to the person in charge. Just remember to ask for an interview even if there are no current openings.

The primary goal of a phone contact is to get an interview. To increase your chances, you need to practice asking for one and have a phone script prepared in advance. Don't be afraid of rejection, and do be prepared to ask for an interview three times. Employers often assume that such a determined person will show the same persistence on the job.

Call each organization and ask to speak to the person who is most likely to hire or supervise you—typically the manager of the business or a department head, *not* the personnel or human resources manager. The following sample telephone script can give you ideas about what to say.

> *"Hello. My name is Pam Nykanen. I am interested in a position in hotel management. I have four years' experience in sales, catering, and accounting with a 300-room hotel. I also have an associate degree in hotel management, plus one year of experience with the Brady Culinary Institute. During my employment, I helped double revenues from meetings and conferences and increased bar revenues by 46 percent. I have good problem-solving skills and am good with people. I am also well-organized, hard working, and detail-oriented. When may I come in for an interview?"*

If you can't get an interview, it never hurts to ask for names of other people who might be able to help you. Add these new referrals to your network, and when you call them, remember to tell them who referred you.

Most Jobs Are with Small Employers

About 70 percent of all people work in small businesses—those with 250 or fewer employees. While the largest corporations have reduced the number of employees, small businesses have been creating as many as 80 percent of the new jobs over the past decade.

Smaller organizations are where most of the job-search action is, so do not ignore this fact. Many opportunities exist to obtain training and promotions in smaller organizations, too. Many do not even have HR departments, so nontraditional job search techniques are particularly effective with them.

E-mail Versus Phone Contact

E-mail offers a variety of advantages over a phone conversation. It's fast, free, and more convenient. You can attach files to it, such as resumes and cover letters, and can forward it to several people at once. Some employers prefer e-mail because they can deal with it on their own schedule.

Many of the major fields discussed in chapter 2 rely on e-mail and Internet communication to do much of their business. This includes the business of hiring employees. For that reason alone, it is important to consider using e-mail contact as an essential strategy in your job search.

E-mail has drawbacks, however. It is easily dismissed or deleted, and e-mails with attachments are viewed with suspicion nowadays. Phone calls, on the other hand, let you interact with employers in a more natural way and provide a more personal touch. Finally, it is much harder for employers to say no to you on the phone when you are requesting an interview.

With all that in mind, you're better off using a combination of the two: e-mailing to reach more people faster and phone calls when you really want to make a connection and land an interview.

STRUCTURE YOUR JOB SEARCH LIKE A JOB

1. **Decide how many hours you will spend a week looking for work.**

   Write here how many hours you are willing to spend each week looking for a job:_____

2. **Decide which days and times you will look for work.**

   Answering the following questions requires you to have a schedule and a plan, just as you had when you were working.

   Which days of the week will you spend looking for a job?

   _____

   How many hours will you look each day?_____

   At what time will you begin and end your job search on each of these days?_____

   _____

3. **Create a specific daily schedule.**

   A specific daily job search schedule is very important because most job seekers find it hard to stay productive each day. You already know which job-search methods are most effective, and you should plan on spending most of your time using those methods.

Getting and Acing Interviews

The average job seeker gets about five interviews a month—fewer than two interviews a week. Yet many job seekers using the techniques we suggest routinely get two interviews a day. But to accomplish this, you must first redefine what an interview is.

The New Definition of an Interview

An interview is *any* face-to-face contact with a person who has the authority to hire or supervise someone with your skills. The person may or may not have an opening at the time.

With this definition, it is *much* easier to get interviews. The key is to interview with all kinds of potential employers, not just those who have job openings. Keep in mind that the hot jobs you are interested in have high growth, so even though a specific employer doesn't have an opening now, they are likely to have one in the very near future. Businesses can't grow without the people needed to run them.

> **Tip:** *Getting two interviews a day equals 10 a week and 40 a month. That's 800 percent more interviews than the average job seeker gets. Who do you think will get a job offer more quickly?*

Do Well in Interviews

No matter how you get an interview, once you are there, you will have to make a good impression. Here are a few quick tips to help you succeed during those crucial 60 minutes.

> **Tip:** *One study indicated that, of those who made it as far as the interview (many others were screened out before then), about 40 percent made a bad first impression, mostly based on their dress and grooming.*

- **Make a good impression before you arrive.** Your resume, e-mails, applications, and other written correspondence create an impression before the interview, so make them professional and error-free.

- **Do some homework on the organization before you go.** You can often get information on a business and on industry trends from the Internet or a library.

- **Dress and groom the same way the interviewer is likely to be dressed—but a little bit better.** Employer surveys find that almost half of all people's dress or grooming creates an initial negative impression. If necessary, get advice on your interviewing outfits from someone who dresses well. Pay close attention to your grooming, too—little things do count.

- **Be early.** Leave in plenty of time to be a few minutes early to an interview.

- **Be friendly and respectful with the receptionist.** Doing otherwise will often get back to the interviewer and result in a quick rejection.

- **Follow the interviewer's lead in the first few minutes.** Even informal small talk can be very important for that person to see how you interact. This is a good time to make a positive comment on the organization or even something you see in the office.

> **Tip:** Your written materials such as cover letters and resumes must be neat and error-free as well, as they also create a first impression.

- **Understand that a traditional interview is not a friendly exchange.** In a traditional interview situation, there is a job opening, and you will be one of several applicants for it. In this setting, the employer's task is to eliminate all applicants but one. The interviewer's questions are designed to elicit information that can be used to screen you out. And your objective is to avoid getting screened out. It's hardly an open and honest interaction, is it?

- **Be prepared to answer the tough interview questions.** Your answers to a few key problem questions may determine whether you get a job offer. There are simply too many possible interview questions to cover one by one. Instead, 10 basic questions cover variations of most other interview questions. So, if you can learn to answer the Top 10 Problem Interview Questions well, you will know how to answer most others.

- **Be prepared for the most important interview question of all.** "Why should I hire you?" is the most important question of all to answer well. Do you have a convincing argument why someone should hire you over someone else? If you don't, you probably won't get that hot job. So think carefully about why someone should hire you and practice your response. Then make sure you communicate this in the interview, even if the interviewer never asks the question in a clear way.

Top 10 Problem Interview Questions

1. Why don't you tell me about yourself?

2. Why should I hire you?

3. What are your major strengths?

4. What are your major weaknesses?

5. What sort of pay do you expect to receive?

6. How does your previous experience relate to the jobs we have here?

7. What are your plans for the future?

8. What will your former employer (or references) say about you?

9. Why are you looking for this type of position, and why here?

10. Why don't you tell me about your personal situation?

The Three-Step Process for Answering Interview Questions

There are thousands of questions that you could be asked in an interview, and there is no way you can memorize a "correct" response for each one. Because interviews are conversational and unpredictable, developing an *approach* to answering an interview question is far more important than memorizing a canned response. The following three-step process can help you fashion an effective answer to most interview questions:

1. **Understand what is really being asked.**

   Most questions are designed to find out about your self-management skills and personality, but interviewers are rarely this blunt. The employer's *real* question is often one or more of the following:

   - Can I depend on you?

   - Are you easy to get along with?

   - Are you a good worker?

   - Do you have the experience and training to do the job if we hire you?

- Are you likely to stay on the job for a reasonable period of time and be productive?

Ultimately, if you don't convince the employer that you will stay and be a good worker, it won't matter if you have the best credentials—he or she won't hire you.

2. **Answer the question briefly in a non-damaging way.** Present the facts of your particular work experience as advantages, not disadvantages. Many interview questions encourage you to provide negative information. Consider the question, "What are your major weaknesses?" This is obviously a trick question, and many people are just not prepared for it.

A good response is to mention something that is not very damaging, such as *"I have been told that I am a perfectionist, sometimes not delegating as effectively as I might."*

But your answer is not complete until you continue with the next step.

3. **Answer the real question by presenting your related skills.** Base your answer on the key skills you have that support the job, and give examples to support these skills. In the previous example (about your need to delegate), a good skills statement might be

"I've been working on this problem and have learned to let my staff do more, making sure that they have good training and supervision. I've found that their performance improves, and it frees me up to do other things."

Whatever your situation, learn to answer questions in a manner that presents you well. It's essential to communicate your skills during an interview, and the three-step process can help you answer problem questions and dramatically improve your responses.

Follow Up on All Contacts

People who follow up with potential employers and with others in their network get jobs faster than those who do not. This is another principle that seems too simple to be so important, but it is true.

We recommend that you send a thank-you note to every person who helps you in your job search and that you do so immediately—within 24 hours of speaking with that person. Sending a thank-you note or e-mail immediately after an interview creates a positive impression and keeps you at the forefront of the employer's mind (ideally, ahead of the other candidates). It also gives you a chance to get in the last word—to include a subtle reminder of why you're the best candidate for the job.

Also send a thank-you e-mail or note to anyone who helps you during your job search. This group of people includes those who give you referrals, people who provide advice, or those who are supportive during your search. You never know when you will need their help again in the future.

Hot Jobs and the Internet

As you look over the jobs in this book, you may notice that many require technical skills, and most require at least a basic comfort level with computers, the Internet, and other technology. Careers in health care, engineering, and information technology often require technical expertise. Even jobs that do not appear technical still call for computer literacy. Most managers in business and finance, for instance, are expected to understand and use spreadsheet, word-processing, and database software.

As a result, it is often taken for granted that job applicants will have these skills and be computer savvy. That applies to the job search and job application process as well. The use of e-mail, electronic resumes, digital portfolios, computerized employment, and especially Internet job posting and aggregator sites continues to grow. And while searching the Internet for job listings and posting your resume on Monster are no substitutes for expanding your network and cold-calling employers, knowing how to use this technology in your job search can drastically improve your chances.

Internet Sites and Aggregators

These Web sites provide listings of job openings and allow you to add your resume for employers to look at. All allow you to look up job openings in a variety of useful ways, including location, job type, and other criteria. Most get their fees from employers and don't charge job seekers.

America's Job Bank—www.americasjobbank2.com. This database includes more than one million job listings from all 50 state employment services, resume-creation and -posting services, and an automated job scout for job seekers. The site was created by the U.S. Public Employment Service. Although public funding recently ended, the site continues to be maintained by the company that has managed it all along, and its services remain free of charge. At this date it is not yet clear whether the new management will attract as many job postings as the site has had in the past.

BestJobsUSA.com—www.bestjobsusa.com. A nice feature here is the state site selection option, which includes a separate jobs page focused on each U.S. state. On each of these pages, you can conduct a job search in only that state and find local articles and information.

CareerBuilder.com—www.careerbuilder.com. This search engine provides access to more than 400,000 job listings. Search by keyword, city, state, field of interest, company, industry, and/or job type; set up a Personal Search Agent to have matching jobs e-mailed directly to your inbox.

CareerShop—www.careershop.com. CareerShop automates the job search and career-management process as much as possible for both job seekers and employers. Search for a job by category, keyword, or location; access career advice; have jobs e-mailed to you weekly; and post your resume online.

FlipDog—www.flipdog.com. Although FlipDog contains the typical options to post your resume, search for jobs, and set up a personal job search agent, job listings here are indexed directly from employers' own Web sites. Search by keyword and location to pull up a list of clickable job titles, each of which directs you to the actual posting on the employer's site.

JobBankUSA.com—www.jobbankusa.com. At JobBankUSA.com's meta-search, in addition to the jobs posted at the site itself, you can run searches in newspapers across the country or through regional job banks, other national and international job banks, and industry-specific job banks. This makes this Web site a useful one-stop shop for searching multiple resources.

Monster—www.monster.com. This is possibly the best-known career site on the Internet. You can post your resume, have jobs e-mailed to you, sign up for e-mail newsletters, and search more than one million monthly job postings. It also includes advice, articles, and tools in an extensive online career center.

NationJob—www.nationjob.com. Search job listings by field, location, duration, educational level, and salary. Register to receive e-mail notification of new jobs matching your criteria. You can also use it to research companies.

Vault.com—www.vault.com. This site provides "insider" information on more than 3,000 companies and 70 industries. Access the "Electronic Water Cooler" to get the scoop from current and former employees at specific companies. Of course, you can also use traditional job bank features such as searchable job postings, an online resume service, e-mail newsletters, and e-mailed job openings.

Yahoo! HotJobs—www.hotjobs.yahoo.com. Browse job postings by category, or search by keyword and location. Post your resume by using the free templates or by uploading your prewritten version to apply online for jobs listed here. You'll also find career articles, resources, and online communities for job seekers.

Aggregator sites. These Internet search engines don't post jobs directly from employers, but instead search other job posting sites and employee sites for all possible jobs that match your search criteria. They collect and repost these job listings with a link to the Internet site they are from. While they don't offer as many services as the sites mentioned earlier, they have the advantage of screening millions of job listings at once. Three of the most popular job aggregator sites are www.simplyhired.com, www.indeed.com, and www.jobster.com.

Using the Internet in Your Job Search

Job seeking on the Internet involves more than simply posting your resume on one or more resume database sites. Here are some other ways the Internet can help you in your job search:

- **Employer Web sites.** Many employers have Web sites that include substantial information plus a list of job openings. Some sites allow you to interact with staff online or via e-mail to get answers to questions about working there.

- **Inside information.** You can use search engines such as Google, Yahoo!, and other Web sites to find information on a specific employer or industry, get job descriptions that list skills and requirements to emphasize in interviews and on your resume, and find career counseling and job search advice.

- **Job boards.** Large national sites such as Monster and HotJobs let you search for openings based on specific criteria.

- **Specialty sites.** You can find Web sites that specialize in the jobs that interest you. Many have job postings, useful information, and access to people in the know. Also, many geographic-specific sites for cities and towns list local openings.

- **E-mail.** Most Internet-savvy employers accept resumes via e-mail, and many will correspond with you this way. Many resume database sites will send you e-mail notices of newly added jobs that meet your criteria.

185

Use Your Resume on the Internet

Most Internet employment sites let you add your resume for free and then charge employers to advertise openings or to search for candidates. Although adding your resume to these databases is not likely to result in job offers, doing so allows you to use your stored resume to easily apply for positions that are posted at these sites. These easy-to-use sites often provide all sorts of useful information for job seekers.

When you post your resume to an online resume database such as Monster, it is stored as a text file with no graphics or other fancy formatting so that it takes up less space and any type of computer can read it. Employers search these text files for keywords that match their requirements for the jobs they have open.

What this means is that the resume you submit online or through e-mail should be in plain text, free of any special formatting. More specifically, the resume that you post online should contain the following:

> **Tip:** The Internet has limitations as a job search tool. While many have used it to get job leads, it has not worked well for far more. Use the Internet in your job search, but plan to use other techniques, including direct contacts with employers, to get the job you want faster.

- No graphics
- No lines
- No bold, italic, or other text variations
- Only one easy-to-scan font (Courier is usually a safe option)
- No tab indents
- No line or paragraph indents

While such resumes look boring, they have the advantage of being universally accepted into company or Web resume databases. Employers also may prefer plain-text files to avoid the risk of viruses that can be transmitted through formatted documents.

For a thorough discussion of resumes with emphasis on the traditional paper-based form, see *Résumé Magic,* by Susan Britton Whitcomb, which is described in the appendix.

The Importance of Keywords

Creating an electronic resume is more involved than just putting it into a plain format. Employers look for qualified applicants in a resume databank by searching for what are called keywords. Your task is to add the right keywords to your electronic resume so that your chance of being selected for appropriate jobs is increased.

Here are some keyword tips for you to keep in mind:

- **Think like a prospective employer.** Think of the jobs you want, and then include the keywords you think an employer would use to find someone who can do what you can do.

- **Review job descriptions from major references.** Read the descriptions for the jobs you seek in major references like the *Occupational Outlook Handbook* or the *O*NET Dictionary of Occupational Titles*. These are available in both print and online formats. They will give you a variety of keywords you can use in your electronic resume.

- **Look for additional sources of keywords to include.** You can identify keywords by reviewing the job descriptions of jobs you want, want ads, employer Web sites, and more.

Always be as specific as possible. Read each job ad carefully, and be ready and willing to make changes to your resume when applying for different positions.

Key Points: Chapter 7

Here are the key points of this chapter:

- Use a variety of job search methods and take an active approach to your job search.

- The two most effective ways of finding job openings are developing a network of contacts and contacting employees directly.

- Redefine what counts as an interview and use a variety of effective job search methods to get two per day.

- Make a good impression in interviews and be certain you can answer the most important question of all: "Why should I hire you?"

- Send an e-mail or handwritten thank-you note within 24 hours of an interview or other networking contact.

- Use e-mail and the Internet to send and post resumes and to further enhance your job search, especially for today's hot jobs.

Appendix

Resources for Job Hunting Plus Background Information

The facts and pointers in this book provide a good beginning to the complex tasks of job choice and employment. If you want additional details, we suggest you consult some of the resources listed here.

Resources for Career Exploration and Decision Making

The *Occupational Outlook Handbook* (**or the** *OOH*): Updated every two years by the U.S. Department of Labor, this book provides descriptions for almost 270 major jobs covering more than 85 percent of the workforce.

The *Enhanced Occupational Outlook Handbook:* Includes all descriptions in the *OOH* plus descriptions of more than 6,300 more-specialized jobs related to them.

The *O*NET Dictionary of Occupational Titles:* The only printed source of the nearly 950 jobs described in the U.S. Department of Labor's Occupational Information Network database. It covers all the jobs in the book you're now reading, but it offers more topics than we were able to fit here.

The *New Guide for Occupational Exploration:* An important career reference that allows you to explore all major O*NET jobs based on your interests.

Overnight Career Choice, by **Michael Farr:** This book can help you choose a career goal based on a variety of criteria, including skills, interests, and values. It is part of the Help in a Hurry series, like the book you're now reading, so it is designed to produce quick results.

Find your state's Web site for accessing labor market information at www.bls.gov/bls/ofolist.htm. Many of these sites have employment projection information for both the state and in-state metropolitan areas.

To compare job opportunities in different states, a valuable site is America's Career InfoNet, at www.acinet.org. Click on "Occupation Profile" and click on "Wages by Occupation and Local Area" (and also "Employment Trends by Occupation"). After you choose an occupation and a state, you'll see the state-specific economic trends for that occupation. Then for most occupations and states there are links that let you compare wages in different regions of the state; compare wages across states; or compare employment trends across states.

Resources for Job Hunting

Job Seeker's Online Goldmine, by **Janet E. Wall, Ed.D.:** This book identifies an impressive array of free and safe Web-based resources that can help you write resumes and find job openings. It also covers Web-based resources that aid in career exploration and paying for education. Free e-mail updates from the author keep the information current.

Seven-Step Job Search: Cut Your Job Search Time in Half, by **Michael Farr:** Still another book in the Help in a Hurry series, this guide expands upon the job-hunting techniques outlined in chapter 7. It includes exercises to help you summarize your skills, experience, and education; build your resume; and organize the job-hunting effort.

Networking for Job Search and Career Success, by **L. Michelle Tullier, Ph.D.:** This is the most comprehensive networking book available and covers the nuts and bolts of how, where, why, and with whom to network. It also addresses the psychological issues such as personality differences and the importance of the right attitude.

Résumé Magic, by **Susan Britton Whitcomb:** Let a professional resume writer show you how to transform your resume into one that gets noticed. Before-and-after examples reveal the techniques that professionals use and the styles that currently are hot.

Where the Information Came From

The information we used in creating this book came mostly from databases created by the U.S. Department of Labor:

- We started with the job information included in the Department of Labor's O*NET (Occupational Information Network) database, which is now the primary source of detailed information on occupations. The Labor Department updates the O*NET on a regular basis, and we used the most recent one available—O*NET release 10.

- We linked the information from the O*NET to several other kinds of data that the U.S. Bureau of Labor Statistics collects: on earnings, projected growth, and number of openings. For data on these topics the BLS uses a slightly different set of job titles than the O*NET uses, so we had to match similar titles.

Of course, information in a database format can be boring and even confusing, so we did many things to help make the data useful and present it to you in a form that is easy to understand.

How Were the 100 Hot Jobs Selected?

Here is the procedure we followed to select the 100 jobs we included in this book:

1. We began with the 949 job titles in the O*NET database. We eliminated 215 jobs because they either are not growing or are expected to have fewer than 500 openings per year or we simply lack data about their projected growth or openings.

2. We eliminated an additional 61 jobs that have average earnings that do not exceed $20,000 per year (or for which we lack earnings data). About 75 percent of wage earners are paid more than $20,000.

3. In order to focus on jobs with high growth or lots of job openings, we retained only jobs that are projected to have *either* at least just shy of 20 percent growth *or* more than 100,000 openings per year. This reduced the list by 536 and left 137 jobs.

4. We dropped an additional 37 jobs because they lack the full range of information—economic topics, work tasks, and work conditions—needed for a reasonably complete description in this book. That left us with 100 hot jobs.

Index

D

E

197

Q–R

S

T–U